"Superpowers" The Missing Dimension In Success!

Mark Edward Duin

Copyright © 2012 Business Without Limits LLC
All rights reserved.
ISBN: 0985453206
ISBN-13: 978-0-9854532-0-6

No part of this publication may be reproduced, stored in a retrieval system, or transmitted, in any form or by any means, electronic, mechanical, photocopying, recording, or otherwise, without the prior written permission of the author or publishers.

This book is sold with the understanding that the author and publisher are not engaged in rendering legal, accounting, counseling, or other professional advice. If legal or other expert assistance is required, the services of a competent professional should be sought. The author, publisher, distributor, or reseller shall have neither liability nor responsibility to any person or entity with respect to any loss or damage caused, or alleged to have been caused, directly or indirectly, by the information contained in this book.

DEDICATION

This book is dedicated to my dad, Dave Duin (D2), whose personal example taught me to never give up on my dreams!

This book is dedicated to everyone who desires more out of life!

This book is dedicated to helping YOU create a rich, fulfilling, rewarding life of true happiness and success!

CONTENTS

Introduction   7

The **SUPERMAN** Formula That Creates Super Success   10

S - Superpowers
- Superpowers of Mortals – Discover What Modern Science and Religious Texts Reveal About Mind Over Matter and Intuition   24

- Higher Power – Prove To Yourself The Existence of a Powerful Force That Can Help You   39

U – Unique Value
- Unique Strengths & Abilities – Discover Your Unique Value And Start Reaping Big Rewards By Benefiting Others   51

- Unique Weakness – Know Your Kryptonite So You Can Minimize The Damage It Causes In Your Life   67

P – Passion and Purpose
- Passion & Purpose – Experience Real Personal Fulfillment and Excitement In Living   80

E – Expertise of Superpowers
- Expertise Of Mind Over Matter – Master The Power Of A Focused Mind So You Can Effect Positive Results In All Areas of Life   97

- Expertise Of Intuition – Develop The Ability To Use Your Intuition To Make Better Decisions And To Heed Internal Warnings!   111

- Expertise of Accessing Higher Power – Experience The Benefit Of Powerful Communication With A Friend In High Places   128

R – Release
- Release Your Internal Enemies – Get Rid of the Negative Subconscious Thinking That Secretly Prevents Your Success   141

M – Make A Difference
- Make A Difference In Your World – Gain A Place In History As A Positive Difference Maker   158

A – Activating Action
- Activate Your Action Plan – Learn To Make Sure You Achieve What You Want   168

N – New Day Every Day
- New Day Every Day – Discover The Easy Way To Ultimate Living A Day At A Time   188

BIBLIOGRAPHY   202

About The Author   204

ACKNOWLEDGMENTS

Special thanks to Zig Ziglar for teaching me that success is the result of a process we can all master! Special thanks to Tom Ziglar for his friendship and willingness to share and advise me. Special thanks to Bill Cashell for showing me how to publish books and use public speaking to make a difference in the lives of others!

Thank you to Bob Goodoien for helping me to believe in myself, and to my Mentor's Leslie Fieger and Robert Stuberg.

I want to acknowledge my loyal wife, our 4 brilliant sons, our family and friends for all their encouragement and support. All of you inspire me to love larger, live more fully, and you keep me striving to make a bigger positive difference in this amazing world!

INTRODUCTION

Most people live their entire lives either searching for something more or resigning themselves to a life unfulfilled. It doesn't have to be that way! The sooner you discover what you're looking for, the better your life will become.

How can this book help you? Ask yourself the following questions and answer each one as honestly as you can. Here goes…

1. Do you want to understand the real causes of success and failure so you can affect more success and happiness in your life?

2. Would you like to uncover your greatest strengths and start capitalizing on them every day from now on?

3. Would you like to understand how your weaknesses are impacting your life and learn effective ways to minimize their damage?

4. Would you like to be free of self-sabotage, past mistakes, regrets, and unproductive negative thinking?

5. Do you want to be recognized for making a positive difference in the world?

6. Would you like to learn the skills that will help you live a meaningful life of purpose and accomplishment?

7. Would you like to start using more of the incredible power of your mind to help you achieve almost anything?

8. Do you want to be excited and enthusiastic about your life?

9. Would you like to develop a habit of being at your best as often as possible?

10. Do you wish you had superpowers that could protect you, guide you, and help you reach your highest potential?

If you answered yes to even a few of these questions you'll find tremendous value in this book. In fact the whole purpose of this writing is to help you achieve a significantly more exciting and fulfilling life!

This powerful book is a little different than most you'll find on the market. It's not written by a PHD with great sounding theories that often don't work in practice. It's also not written by a Spiritual Guru who may not be tuned-in to the reality you face every day.

I am simply a former 9th grade dropout drug addict and street dweller, who's found a way to live that brings great accomplishment, fulfillment, and happiness. I've literally come from scrounging on the streets for survival and sleeping in the park to providing technical expertise to Fortune 500 and Fortune 50 Companies.

Today I am a respected life improvement author, an award winning public speaker, a personal, career, and business success coach, and the founder of Business Without Limits, LLC. All ventures dedicated to helping people become their personal best. Beyond business and financial success I enjoy a successful long-standing marriage and family life.

I've had to overcome incredible obstacles and great odds to arrive at the fantastic life I am experiencing. I know for a fact that no matter who you are, no matter what your life has been like, your life can be much more than it is! Your potential is indeed incredible!

If you're trying to find your way to a better life this book won't just show you the way, it will take you to it. The valuable tools you need are now in your hands. Get ready for some powerful positive changes!

My deepest desire, my prayer, my hope and faith is that you will find everything you need to achieve the fantastic life you are capable of. Follow the steps in this book with the full expectation that you will achieve life transforming results, and you surely will!

S – Superpowers

Chapter 1: "The SUPERMAN Formula That Creates Super-Success"

"To accomplish great things, we must not only act, but also dream, not only plan, but also believe." - Anatole France 1844-1924, French Novelist

The Superhero

Superheroes provide a great analogy for understanding what our incredible human potential is all about. Being a Superhero would be awesome! Just think of the advantages you'd have. For starters you would already know your life purpose, your Destiny. No wasting time trying to figure out what to do with your life.

Your sole purpose in life would be to go around using your unique talents and abilities to serve others and to help make the world a better place for everyone. Not only would you have a purpose in life you would understand the real power of your unique abilities and you would be busy enjoying a life that provides incredible value to others.

It would probably feel pretty good to rack up incredible feats and accomplishments every day. At the end of your days (if Superheroes died) you could look back with deep satisfaction, knowing you made a difference in the lives of countless individuals. You actually helped change the world for the better.

Can you imagine knowing your purpose in life? Understanding your greatest abilities and knowing how to use them to provide value to others. If you had access to real superpowers you'd possess powerful resources to solve problems and overcome obstacles. You'd be able to break through limitations advancing far beyond mediocre living.

Superhero's to the Rescue

Have you ever noticed how Superman has his own unique characteristics? He can fly of course. I don't think anybody can change clothes as fast as he can. He can see through walls, leap tall buildings in a single bound, and he's faster than a speeding bullet. He provides his own unique value to the world by using his own unique gifts, gifts that make him different than any other superhero. His value is different than Batman's.

Batman on the other hand uses technology to get the job done because he doesn't really possess superpowers other than ingenuity. He's got the bat-mobile, bat-copter, bat-bike and all sorts of helpful gadgets. Both of these heroes are uniquely super. All day every day they look for opportunities to use their unique abilities to benefit others and make life better for everyone. The real world sure could use a few good Superheroes!

Superhero Living

You may not have realized it before but you do have the potential to live the rewarding life of a superhero. You have unique talents, abilities, skills, genetics and life experiences that can benefit others.

If you're like most people you probably don't even understand just how valuable you are. How do I know you're so valuable? Because every person has almost unlimited potential, everyone is a superhero waiting to emerge.

I know that if I can come from a life of no value, living on the streets, tormented by addiction, uneducated, with no friends and no hope, to a life of success fulfillment and purpose, anyone else can too.

Every person I've ever met, from the street dweller to Fortune 50 executive has something of value that can benefit others. You are no different. You're just as unique as any superhero. If only you had the superpowers to go with your human uniqueness, then you could really get things done? Fret not mortal, you actually do have incredible superpowers and you'll be discovering them shortly.

The Road Less Travelled

Few have discovered the way to a fulfilling exciting and meaningful life. Few have invested even a little of their valuable time to discover the way. You're about to break loose from the unfulfilled masses and discover a life far above what you've settled for in the past.

You're about to embark on the road less traveled, the life of the admired respected and desired Superhero. You are about to discover the great potential inside of you that's waiting for the chance to break out and shine.

The SUPERMAN Formula for Super-Living

The following outline is an introduction to what you'll be learning in the fascinating chapters of this book. You'll be introduced to the SUPERMAN formula for Super-Living.

In order to maximize the benefits you'll be receiving, I recommend reading each chapter in order and doing the exercises as you encounter them. Each chapter builds upon the last. The more you fully engage and participate in this life changing process the more your life will change for the better.

This book is divided into 8 sections that spell out SUPERMAN. The SUPERMAN acronym stands for:

S-Superpowers – Gain Understanding of the Power Available to Change Your Life for The Better

U-Unique Talent and Ability – Discover Your Unique Value to the World

P- Passion and Purpose – The Foundation of an Exciting and Meaningful Life

E- Expertise in Superpowers – Gaining Expertise in the Skills You Need to Succeed

R- Release – Gain Freedom from Worry, Fear, Guilt, and Regret

M- Make a Difference – Giving that Blesses You and Others

A- Action - Take Positive Action Even When You don't Feel like It

N- New Day Every Day– Start every day with a Routine for Super-Living

Let's take a brief look at these sections to gain a better understanding of what's ahead.

Superpowers

S stands for SUPERPOWERS. Life is full of challenges, not only do you face your own limitations you have to deal with many unwanted circumstances and obstacles throughout your life. You never know what you're going to encounter. That's why you need to understand your options.

You need to understand the sources of real power available to help you through life's journey. If you ever hope to go beyond mediocre living you'll want all the help you can get. Lucky for you there's an enormous amount of power available to help you soar through life. You can count on power for direction, inspiration, wisdom, and anything else that's in support of fulfilling your highest potential.

In this section on "Superpowers" you'll gain a deeper understanding of the extraordinary human abilities of mind over matter and intuition. Abilities every human is born with and that almost anyone can learn to use and develop. We'll explore what these abilities are, how they work, potential applications, and their limitations. We will also look at the scientific understanding of what these capabilities are and how they work in humans.

Even though human abilities are great indeed, sometimes they are not enough. For this reason we'll also explore the existence of a Higher Power for effecting good in our lives. In fact, you'll actually have a chance to begin proving to yourself the existence of a Higher Power that you can access for help and direction.

Unique Talent & Ability

U stands for UNIQUE Talent and Ability. No one has ever existed throughout eternity that is exactly like you. No one in the future will ever be exactly like you. You are it. You are a magnificent and rare one of a kind creation. No person has your exact combination of natural talents, learned skills, life experience or abilities. No one looks at things the same way you do. You have a unique perspective and that's valuable. In this section you will discover your greatest strengths so you can begin to find ways to capitalize on them every day.

Being human you also possess at least a few weaknesses. Even if you become the most highly skilled person on the planet, one weakness uncontrolled has the potential to destroy you. Being aware of your weaknesses will allow you to minimize the negative impact they have on your life.

By developing and using your strengths and minimizing your weaknesses you will greatly increase your quality of life and your value to the world. This section will help you understand your unique value. You'll engage in a fun and powerful discovery of your abilities so you can begin putting them to better use right away.

Passion & Purpose

P stands for PASSION & PURPOSE. Everybody needs something to be passionate about. Passion gives us drive. Without passion life is monotonous boring and dull. Without it we can exist but we can never excel. Passion motivates us, energizes us, and helps us to relentlessly pursue the things we want. Passion adds excitement to living and makes life fun. It turns on the energizer bunny inside of us.

When you identify the things you are passionate about it will point you toward a meaningful purpose for your life. Having a meaningful purpose will give you a reason to get up every day, something exciting and fun to focus on.

Passion and Purpose go hand in hand and are necessary ingredients if you want to break out of the rut of mediocre living. In this section you'll discover your hidden passions and you'll begin to map out a vision for yourself that will add incredible meaning and fulfillment to your life.

Expertise in Superpowers

E stands for EXPERTISE. Knowledge is power. The more you know the more you can do and the more you can do the more you can accomplish. There's no need for any human being to be ordinary because we all have the capability to be extraordinary. You'll definitely want to develop some level of proficiency with the skills addressed in this section.

In this section you'll learn some practical uses for the abilities of mind over matter and intuition and how to apply these skills in your daily life.

You will be shown some simple methods for developing your own superhuman abilities including several do it yourself experiments for testing and developing these fascinating human powers.

In this section you'll also learn some powerfully effective methods of accessing a Higher Power so you can seek wisdom, guidance, direction and help to achieve your highest potential. Gaining expertise in these skills will serve you well and will provide tremendous value to others all the days of your life.

Release

R stands for RELEASE. Could you be sabotaging yourself? You can trace the lives of the most successful people on earth and you'll notice some very definite patterns. The same is true of those who are not successful in life. Examine anyone who lives their entire life in failure and you'll note their lives also are full of patterns. We need to understand the patterns that have led to our successes and those that have caused us to fail. The good news is that we have the ability to change; we don't have to stay stuck in the same patterns forever.

As you identify destructive behaviors in your life you can choose to eliminate them. If you never examine yourself, you're doomed to repeat the same mistakes over and over again. That's why you need to identify your problem areas and get rid of them. Your mind is indeed a powerful tool for good, but sometimes you use it against yourself without even realizing it.

Your subconscious mind can harbor fears, doubts, anger, self-pity, regrets, and lack of confidence. All these things hold you back from getting where you want to be.

You can say positive affirmations all you want, but what you really think about yourself at the deepest levels is what affects your behavior. Deep down you know everything you have ever done, both good and bad. If you haven't fully forgiven yourself, you are potentially preventing yourself from moving on to greater things.

Once you destroy your internal enemies your whole world opens up. An incredible sense of freedom and a new lease on life fills your entire being. You simply must release any self-sabotage that exist within you.

Until you get rid of these hidden negative thoughts you will be limited. In this section you'll learn to discover and release the enemies you have within. If you don't do anything else in this book please do the things outlined in this chapter. This technique alone will afford you an incredible freedom you need to experience.

Make a Difference

M stands for MAKING A DIFFERENCE. "You reap what you sow" this is a universal law that has proven itself true time and time again. There are two basic approaches to life, the way of giving and the way of getting. An attitude of getting is an empty illusion.

People often think that the more stuff they can get the better they'll feel, but getting more stuff doesn't work very well. It leaves you feeling empty all too soon. That's why you want to get more stuff. Once you understand that getting is not fulfilling you can begin to focus on something that is fulfilling, and that is giving.

Giving is fulfilling there's no way around it. When you find a way to use your unique abilities to benefit others you'll feel good inside. You'll discover that you're actually happier when you're giving than when you're receiving. You need to provide value to others in order to feel fulfilled.

All the more reason to strive for superhero status. When your motivation for doing anything is to give, you're on the right track. Real rewards are the result. Not temporary or unfulfilling rewards, but real deep and meaningful rewards. Rewards that last a lifetime.

Once you've progressed to this chapter you'll have already begun to make an incredible difference in your own life. Actually you'll have already begun to have a positive effect on others as well.

Remember, you want to fulfill your highest potential. In this section you'll see examples of real people who have made an incredible difference in the world. You'll learn to constantly be on the lookout for opportunities to provide your unique value to the world and as a result you'll continue to grow to your most fulfilling potential.

Action

A is for ACTION. Nothing good happens without forward movement. Do you ever find it hard to make yourself do what you know you should be doing? Face it, we're still regular humans (for now). Being human makes us prone to inaction from time to time.

No matter what we know we should be doing, we often have a hard time making ourselves do it. We know we should exercise and eat right. We know we should be honest. We know we should be better with our money. We know that if we did all the things we knew were good for us we would be much better off in life.

The challenge is to find a way to make ourselves do the things we need to do. So, why don't we do the things we need to do? We have a plethora of reasons, or should I say excuses. Fear of failure, fear of success, lack of confidence, lack of ability and anything else we can think of to hold ourselves back. We absolutely must learn to make ourselves do what needs to be done in order to succeed. We have to recognize when we're preventing ourselves from moving ahead and we need to do something about it quickly.

Fortunately there are a good number of practical techniques and tricks for helping you get into action. When you combine the techniques you'll learn in this section with the superpowers available to you, you'll have a winning combination.

In this section we'll focus on how to stay in constant positive action so you can achieve the life you really want. You'll be learning some simple methods you can apply for those times when you don't feel like moving forward.

New Day Every Day

N stands for NEW DAY. Every day is a new day. Daily movement in the right direction will add up to a lifetime of success.

Making progress toward your passion and purpose a little each day will make life exciting and worthwhile. One positive day at a time you can look back and see that you've done something of value, something you feel good about. Now that's a great way to live each day. The value you offer the world every day creates an incredible amount of value to the world over the long run.

Your time is your life. What you do in the time you have is the key to your success. In this section you'll be shown how to develop your own workable daily routine. A practice designed to keep you progressing toward your incredible potential. This process will guarantee that you make every day count so you can experience a great life of satisfaction. In the process you will become the ultimate you, fulfilling your incredible superhuman potential.

Following the SUPERMAN formula will enable you to achieve your superhuman potential. This formula will give you access to real superpowers for change. It will help you understand your unique talents and abilities and the value you have to offer the world. It will help you discover passion and a purpose for living so you can live an exciting life with real meaning. It will provide you with expertise in skills that will propel you far beyond ordinary existence.

The SUPERMAN formula enables you to release the enemies within so you can experience freedom and hope for the future. It will show you how to make an incredible difference in the lives of others and in the world you live in.

It will help you take action no matter what, making procrastination a thing of the past. It will provide a way to enjoy each new day, pursuing excellence the rest of your days. A way to live every day as a superhero, racking up a lifetime of valuable meaningful accomplishment and success. The SUPERMAN formula will reshape your life into real Super-Living.

Circumstances & Obstacles Can't Stop You

Make no mistake, almost like clockwork as soon as you start moving toward the things you desire, obstacles will magically appear. Its life's little way of testing how badly you want something.

Always remember, if you want anything bad enough you will find the way to achieve it.

The important thing to understand about obstacles is that you have to find the way around them in order to advance to the next level of success. With every obstacle there is a way to the other side. For those who find the way around their obstacles the rewards are great indeed, for those who don't the penalty can be harsh!

Here's an example of what I mean. Two people experience separate tragic accidents and both become amputees. One gives up and lives a miserable existence the rest of their days. This person becomes resentful unproductive and dissatisfied with life, eventually becoming a burden on society.

The other person gets the powerful help they need and learns to walk using a prosthesis. After a while this person learns to run and before long can run a marathon. After this individual's marathon accomplishment, they write a book on overcoming adversity. Finally this hero becomes a motivational speaker and a mentor to others who have experienced a similar tragedy.

Which one of these people will look back over their life with satisfaction, feeling great about their accomplishments and the contributions they made? Which one will live a more happy productive and meaningful life? And let's not forget about all the people who would receive help from the successful amputee. Where would they be without the inspirational life that touched them?

We can't always control circumstances but we can control what we do with the circumstances we are given. Finding the solution to an obstacle is never as hard as we imagine it to be. Never fool yourself into giving up on your dreams, there is plenty of help available to get you to the other side of your obstacles.

There's no time to waist. There really is no reason why you can't live an exciting, successful, superhero life. Grab a pair of tights and a cape (just kidding) and get ready to blast off. You are about to embark on the greatest adventure of your life. In fact, from this point on your life will be an incredibly exciting and rewarding adventure.

"Most people never run far enough on their first wind to find out if they've got a second. Give your dreams all you've got and you'll be amazed at the energy that comes out of you." - William James 1842-1910, American Philosopher

Chapter 2: "Superpowers of Mortals – Discover What Modern Science and Religious Texts Reveal About Mind Over Matter & Intuition"

Extraordinary Human Powers

Ordinary human powers are certainly impressive all by themselves. We have far greater ability than any other creature on the planet. Our intellectual power and unique physical design provide us with tremendous capabilities. Not only can we create things with our minds, we can implement them with our fingers. Much more advanced than an ape to be sure.

We have the ability to research and study information, the ability to reason and come up with creative ideas. We can apply our knowledge in concrete ways. That's pretty powerful. However, we possess even greater abilities than these.

Phrases that sum up the incredible power of the human mind are common. A multitude of book titles and positive sayings reflect this truth. "Think and Grow Rich", "The Power of Positive Thinking", "The Magic of Thinking Big", "Whatever You Believe You Can Achieve", notice any trends here? Yes the power of the human mind is well recognized although it is also often misunderstood. Let's take a look at just how powerful your mind really is.

Mind Over Matter

Using deep concentration and physical technique, a martial arts Master can break a board or even a concrete block with their head. Ouch!

Top athletes often use techniques of mind over matter to push themselves to incredible limits. Skate boarders seem to defy the laws of physics all the time and live to tell about it. These examples all represent forms of mind over matter. The humans in these examples use the power of focused concentration to accomplish incredible physical acts the majority of us would never dare try.

Mind over matter has often played a role in physical healing. There are many reported cases of unconventional healing around the globe. Miraculous healing has taken place for individuals across multiple religions, and even for people of no religion. Some have even been healed of serious illness simply by taking a placebo, a sugar pill. Their minds believe they're taking something that will cure them, and their body responds.

Eastern Practitioners of energy healing provide another example of how the mind can be used to affect matter. They direct energy, via thought, to cause healing in their patients. Energy healers who practice Qi-gong and Reiki are becoming more accepted by the Western Medical community because of the evidence of their effectiveness.

I recently heard about a person in the hospital in the Midwest with an infection in his leg. During his stay, the hospital had an energy healer come in and focus energy on the wound. Many American nurses have taken classes on Reiki energy healing.

When we consider how the mind affects healing, we need to consider that there are actually multiple minds involved. There is the mind of the healer of course, and the mind of the patient. When a patient truly believes (deep in their mind and heart) they will be healed, miracles happen!

I find it interesting that the great Nazarene, after healing someone, would say, "Your faith has made you well." He sure could have said "I made you well", "The power of God has made you well" or just plain "You have been made well". He seemed to make a point of saying, "Your faith has made you well". He implied that the faith or belief of the person being healed had a lot to do with them being healed.

Another interesting statement he made was, "I tell you the truth, if you have faith as small as a mustard seed, you can say to this mountain, "Move from here to there and it will move. Nothing will be impossible for you." The power of what our minds believe is indeed impressive.

Psycho-kinesis is a scientific term used to describe advanced mind over matter capability. People with this highly developed ability can actually move objects with their mind. "Look mom no hands!" Sorry I couldn't help myself. Yes real people have been scientifically observed moving objects with their mind. Many in this field of study believe all people can develop this ability to some degree. Affecting matter with thought, mind over matter, is an interesting prospect indeed.

The possibilities are great. By controlling and focusing our thoughts we could improve our performance in many areas. This applies at work, at home, in sports, self-healing, in the achievement of goals and in self-improvement to name a few. Yes the proper focus of our minds can be used to take us far beyond where we would normally go. We'll take a look at some practical applications for using mind over matter a little later on.

Human Intuition the Sixth Sense

Intuition is another curious power we humans possess. Intuition or psychic ability is the ability to receive information by some means other than our normal five senses. A sixth sense if you will. Sometimes we just have a gut feel about something and our feeling ends up being right on the money.

Some people learn to listen to their gut feelings and actually use them to make critical decisions. Logic and reason have traditionally been the tools of choice for making decisions, but logic and reason rely on complete and factual information. How often is that fully available? Gut feelings can often add another dimension to making sound decisions.

What we typically refer to as intuition is actually on the very low end of the sixth sense scale. A more highly developed sixth sense is often referred to as psychic ability. Most of us have experienced knowing something through our sixth sense. We may think of someone we haven't thought about in ten years, and the next day we run into them at a store. Why did this person come to mind totally out of the blue in advance of this meeting? It seems a little peculiar when these types of things happen but we usually don't give them a second thought.

On the other hand, when it comes to more highly developed psychic ability, most of us are still forming our opinions. Whatever we think about it, almost everyone will agree there is something to this sixth sense business, even if we don't fully understand it yet.

Many experiments have proven the sixth sense is real. Remote viewing is a scientific term used for the ability to receive information intuitively over a distance. Several government's including our own, have performed numerous experiments using remote viewing, with some impressive results. Russell Targ a physicist, PHD, and co-author of the book "Miracles of the Mind", was heavily involved with these types of experiments and does an outstanding job of describing them in his book.

Mr. Targ outlines a number of these "remote viewing" experiments. In some cases an individual was given the longitude and latitude coordinates to a site they had never seen before, they were then asked to remotely view the location with their mind and report what they found. A number of individuals were able to describe sites very accurately. Their accuracy was confirmed by satellite photography.

In one reported case, information gathered via remote viewing pertained to a specific object inside of a building. The object was unable to be seen by satellite. It was only after some time that the building was explored; confirming that what the remote viewer had seen was indeed accurate. Talk about x-ray vision, I'm not even sure Superman could look through buildings halfway across the world.

Many people involved with these experiments believe that everyone has this ability and is capable of developing it to a greater degree. As an interesting side note, there also seems to be evidence to suggest that if this ability is used for purely selfish gain, it doesn't work. That in itself is interesting. It's almost as if the capability has been built into humans and a moral power oversees its use to ensure we don't abuse it, that's pretty cool.

Although remote viewing is an ability that can be learned, it's not 100% accurate or consistent. Some people seem to be able to remote view better than others. It appears that the more common ability of plain old intuition has the greatest potential for practical use for most of us. Things like getting a bad feeling about going somewhere and deciding not to go, then later learning that something bad happened where you were supposed to be.

Yes an early warning system could be useful. Intuition can also provide us with little insights here and there. Many company executives make very good decisions based on their gut feelings.

How Human Superpowers Work!

You may have to read this section over several times to better understand what's being described. The science of Quantum Physics and the theory of the Holographic Universe are indeed mind bending subjects. However a brief understanding of some of their basic concepts will go a long way in understanding how Mind Over Matter and Intuition work. So just how do these amazing abilities work?

Scientists in the area of Quantum Physics have come to the conclusion that all things are made of energy. In fact the Chinese word for Physics is "Wu Li", which can be translated as "patterns of organic energy." In simplest terms, physical things (made up of matter) are not really solid. They are made up of patterns of energy that appear to us as solid. If matter is truly made up of patterns of energy rather than a solid mass, it's a little easier to understand how thought waves (energy waves of thought) could actually affect and interact with matter (other energy patterns).

Another interesting scientific find is that subatomic particles appear to have intelligence of their own. Photons (subatomic particles) seemingly can predict what type of experiment will be taking place and respond accordingly.

In 1982 at the University of Paris, a research team led by physicist Alain Aspect conducted one of the 20th Centuries most significant experiments. Aspect's team discovered that under certain circumstances subatomic particles are able to instantaneously communicate with each other over a distance, regardless if they are 10 feet or 10 billion miles apart.

You and I and everything else are made up of atoms containing subatomic particles. If the subatomic particles of an energy pattern, (physical thing or matter) are somehow able to communicate with other subatomic particles that are located far away, that would go a long way in explaining phenomenon such as intuition and mind over matter.

For thousands of years Eastern Mystics have said that the world is made of energy. Science has confirmed it. Maybe there is something to meditating on mountain tops after all. Let's take a look at the correlation between mind and matter (energy).

It's important to understand how our human minds interact with the world around us if we want to affect positive change in our lives. Here's my layman's attempt to summarize how the mind interacts with and has an effect on matter...

Everything in our world is made up of patterns of intelligent energy, or matter. All matter consists of atoms that are made up of subatomic particles with a lot of space in between them. Subatomic particles are constantly moving around. Movement produces energy; therefore everything is made up of pulsating, vibrating energy. Movement produces frequency waves of energy (vibrations).

Our thoughts also produce energy waves, known as thought waves. When our thoughts are focused and fully charged with intense desire and emotion, powerful thought waves radiate out from us and actually collide with and have an effect on other energy patterns.

In the case of psychic ability or intuition we may consider that a psychic is somehow able to tune into the vibrating intelligent information contained in the matter of someone or something else and is able to interpret the intelligent information being transmitted by the pulsating waves of energy.

One theory, the Universal Mind Theory, explains it in the following way. Information is stored in everything around us throughout space and time. The human brain acts as a transmitter and a receiver. As a receiver the human brain can tune into information across space and time, receive it and interpret it. The more emotionally charged the information is the stronger its transmission and the easier it is to receive.

This Universal Mind Theory or something like it could account for many otherwise unexplainable phenomenon. Here's an example; a person senses something has gone terribly wrong with their son or daughter. Moments later they receive a phone call telling them their son or daughter has been in a car accident. The five physical senses are not at all in play here, only the sixth sense. The parent in this case was somehow able to tune-in to the highly emotionally charged thoughts transmitted from their child as the traumatic accident occurred.

These types of things actually happen to a good number of people who are not considered psychics. They're just average people like you and I. This train of thought explains how the ability of mind over matter works. If all things are energy including our thoughts, highly focused and emotionally charged thought waves would be able to project outside of us and interact with other minds and objects.

Again, as the great Nazarene said, "Your faith has made you well" and "I tell you the truth, if you have faith as small as a mustard seed, you can say to this mountain, move from here to there and it will move. Nothing will be impossible for you."

Watch What You Think

With this understanding we need to consider that our subconscious mind is working 24 hours a day, constantly broadcasting thought waves that affect everything around us. A positive mindset at the subconscious level is critical for affecting positive results in our lives. If our minds are continuously charged with powerful positive thoughts, we will literally be positively affecting ourselves and everything around us.

On the flip side, if we're constantly focused on negative thoughts and pessimism, we negatively affect ourselves and everything around us.

Have you ever been in a room with someone who was in a great mood? Everyone in that room is positively charged by the experience. The opposite is also true. When we encounter someone who is intensely negative it drags us down. It drains the life right out of us. We literally get good or bad vibes from people places and things. That's why it's critically important to be aware of what we allow to enter our minds, both at a conscious and subconscious level. Garbage in garbage out as they say.

Focusing your mind to positively affect your life is the most useful application for your human superpowers. In the chapter on "Expertise in Superpowers" you'll learn how to do just that.

The Golden Rule

Now that we have a reasonable handle on our incredible human abilities and an understanding of how we interact with the world around us, we can take a look at the rules that apply to success or failure in life. What I'm really talking about here is the law of cause and effect. I like to call it "The Law of the Boomerang," meaning, what you send out returns to you with multiplied strength.

This applies to everything you think, say, or do. For example if you think negatively towards anyone, they can sense it and think negatively in return. If you say or do something negative or damaging towards others, you can be sure it will come back to haunt you at some point.

The reason it seems to come back with multiplied strength is because we also know deep down that we have done wrong. We now receive the negative thoughts feeling and emotions of others towards us, as well as our own negative thoughts feelings and emotions toward ourselves. It's difficult to live a successful and happy life if much of what we think say and do comes back to bite us.

On the other hand, if we think say and do positive things towards others, positive thoughts words and actions will return to us. We also experience the benefit of our own positive thoughts feelings and emotions towards ourselves because we feel good about doing good. If we're going to be happy and successful we need to live by the golden rule.

From this point on strive to think speak and act towards others exactly as you would have them think speak and act toward you. As you are about to discover through the following simple exercise, obeying this one simple rule will have dramatically positive effects on your life.

Simple Mind Over Matter Exercise

Here's a practical way to use mind over matter to affect positive change in your life over the next seven days. Use the following exercise to put yourself into a highly productive and positive frame of mind. You'll be amazed at the positive rewards you'll receive in return for adjusting your thinking.

A little later on in this book we'll be exploring some more advanced mind over matter methods along with some great techniques for developing and applying your intuitive abilities.

Do the following 3 exercises to the best of your ability over the next seven days and see how they affect you and the people and situations around you.

Exercise Number 1:

First, copy the 3 statements listed below on a piece of paper. You may want to do this in your own handwriting. For the next 7 days as soon as you wake up, then during the middle of your day, and right before you go to bed read or speak these 3 statements.

Smile as you read or speak each statement and try to feel the emotion of each statement. Repeat them over and over creating a rhythm as you repeat them. You'll notice that after repeating them you'll begin to feel what each statement says.

It's amazingly powerful for such a simple exercise. This is a great way to begin and end each day. It only takes a few short minutes but it powerfully tunes your mind to an optimum state.

Go ahead and try it, give yourself a boost right now. Read through each statement very quickly. Speak them out loud if at all possible as this seems to add power to the process.

- I am Strong, Positive, Happy and Fun. I am Strong, Positive, Happy and Fun. I am Strong, Positive, Happy and Fun. I am Strong, Positive, Happy and Fun. I am Strong, Positive, Happy and Fun. I am Strong, Positive, Happy and Fun. I am Strong, Positive, Happy and Fun.

- I am Super Successful in everything I do. I am Super Successful in everything I do. I am Super Successful in everything I do. I am Super Successful in everything I do. I am Super Successful in everything I do. I am Super Successful in everything I do. I am Super Successful in everything I do.

- All blockages, obstacles and troubles removed. All blockages, obstacles and troubles removed. All blockages, obstacles and troubles removed. All blockages, obstacles and troubles removed. All blockages, obstacles and troubles removed. All blockages, obstacles and troubles removed. All blockages, obstacles and troubles removed.

Notice how you feel after repeating these statements. Stick with this exercise 3 times a day for the next 7 days and I guarantee you'll start seeing some positive results.

Throughout the day, whenever you're alone, walking, waiting, or taking a quick break, and again just as you drift off to sleep, repeat these statements over and over in your mind. The more often you repeat them the more powerful their affect will be on you. When your mind is trained to focus on positive thoughts and feelings the majority of your day, very positive things begin to happen!

Exercise Number 2:

Be aware of your posture throughout the day: Stand tall, sit up straight, and walk with purpose. Whenever you catch yourself slumping over or walking without vigor, snap into a strong positive physical posture. This practice will help you look and feel more confident and positive and others will notice it too.

Exercise Number 3:

Watch your interaction: Smile at others, use a firm handshake, listen intently to others and strive to talk about things that are of interest to them. Treat every person like they are the most important person you've met.

Listen, pay attention, show respect and appreciation to every person you meet. Look at every person as a deeply loved brother or sister, father or mother, son or daughter. Rank the needs of others as equal to your own, remember that we're all in this life together. As you do these things positive rewards will return to you with multiplied strength.

These 3 simple exercises will show you how the focus of your mind actually affects the matter in your body and the matter outside of you.

When you take control of your mind and focus it on the right things, good things happen. If you don't take control of your mind you'll find that it often leads you where you don't want to go.

Accessing Higher Power

So far we've examined how our minds interface with the physical world around us. In the next chapter we'll explore the possibility of interfacing with a higher power (often referred to as God or The Universal Intelligence).

What if the transmitter and receiver in your mind is also the method used for communication to and from an intelligent higher source of knowledge and wisdom? Have you ever found yourself in an impossible situation? A situation where only God himself could help you? You take that rare chance and cry out in your mind, praying with all your might. An intense, heartfelt, energized prayer for help?

Almost immediately the situation or problem begins to take care of itself. The possibility of being able to interact with the most powerful force in existence is certainly something worth exploring further.

The incredible human powers of mind over matter and intuition, even in the most highly developed individuals are not 100 percent accurate or consistent. Although these abilities are indeed powerful and can provide tremendous value to our lives, they are not the end all.

That's precisely why we will want to explore the possibility of interfacing with an all-powerful force for good. In the next chapter you will be able to prove for yourself whether or not an all-powerful, all-knowing force for good exists or not.

Chapter 3: "Higher Power – Prove To Yourself The Existence Of A Powerful Force That Can Help You!"

What's a Person to Believe?

To believe or not to believe, that is the question? Is it better to believe in a power greater than ourselves or not? Could there be any benefit to believing in an all-powerful force for good? Is there any downside? I guess another question would be, is there any upside to not believing in an all-powerful force for good? And what would be the downside to not believing?

Having access to the highest power in the entire universe would be the absolute best possibility imaginable. Imagine for a moment an incredible all-powerful force that is pure love, all-knowing, all-powerful and that truly wants only the best for you. If this force or being actually exists and is available to help you through your life journey, what could be better than that?

The Separation Between God and Religion

For the sake of this conversation let's make a separation between God and religion. The reason I say this is because religion can often be confusing, controversial, and seemingly contradicting, all symptoms of human involvement.

However I would like to point out that the principles of religion are good and for everyone's benefit. For example, If the human race would obey just two of the ten biblical Commandments, the entire world would benefit greatly. Let's say that everyone in the world decided to obey the commands of "do not steal" and "do not kill".

If all mankind obeyed only these two Commandments, the entire world economy would greatly improve because of the lack of theft. Prisons would empty out solving the overcrowding problem. You could leave your car and home unlocked at all times and you would feel safe walking through any neighborhood in the world. Everyone in the world would greatly benefit as a result of only obeying two out of ten of these commands.

The problem with religion is not the principles they teach, it's with our ability and willingness to practice the principles they teach. It's not hard to imagine that these lofty principals of religion could have come from a higher source than faulty human beings. When we examine our bloody human history and our inhumanity towards one another it's difficult to imagine that we humans were ever capable of coming up with the fantastic principals offered in religion.

It is entirely possible that these could have come from something more highly advanced than we are. At least we would have to admit it's possible that something greater than humans originated the principals we find in our religions. Principals that if practiced would benefit all of mankind.

If indeed there is a higher force for good, wouldn't it stand to reason that this force would want to help you experience the best life for you? Again I'm not talking about following or not following any particular religion. I'm talking about exploring the possibility of communicating with the highest force for good and asking it to guide you into living the life that is truly best for you.

Religion is a touchy subject as we can observe by all the wars and killing that have resulted from them over the centuries. People of all religions and even people of no religion have experienced miracles. Everyone claims that theirs is the only true religion.

Let's leave religion out of it for now and look at this topic of a higher power from a different point of view. Let's explore this from the standpoint of the positive results we get in our lives. Can belief in a higher power for good improve the results of our lives and what are the pros and cons of believing or not believing in a higher power for good?

Benefits of Belief

Positive results, that's what we're looking for. So how would we benefit from belief in a higher power for good? What's in it for us? First off, believing in a higher power would imply that there is something greater than the physical us. That's actually encouraging to me.

Belief in a higher power would provide hope for mankind, for us individually, and especially for those who have no hope at all. Comfort in time of need would be another plus. There are so many things we don't have answers to, so trusting in something higher up could be a benefit as we try to figure it all out.

Another benefit to belief in a higher power is the necessity for a higher standard of living. The concept of right and wrong would help us focus on personal accountability, accountability to ourselves, to our fellow human beings and to our environment. Our behavior should improve because we would be striving to do what we believe is right.

Some improved behaviors would include deliberately striving not to lie, not to cheat, not stealing and not harming others. We benefit because we have a clear conscience. Others would benefit too for obvious reasons.

That's not all bad. If this higher power turned out to be real and truly did have our best interest at heart, we could develop a connection with it and gain access to this higher power for effecting good results in our lives. Okay there are some potential benefits to us if we choose to believe in something greater.

Downside to Belief

So what's the downside to believing in a higher force for good? Worst-case we could potentially have wasted a little time believing in something that doesn't exist. Even though we still really receive benefit from believing in it anyway. After all when we believe in something, to us It Is Real!

Another downside is that we could potentially be giving credit for the good in our lives to something that doesn't exist. I don't know about you but I can live with that, especially if my life is improving.

As long as we don't get sidetracked by human religious interpretations, there really doesn't appear to be a whole lot of downside to believing in a higher power for good. If this higher power does exist the upside could be huge.

Benefits to Disbelief

Not believing in a higher power should have its own set of positives, right?

So let's take a look at this. Okay, we don't believe there's some higher force for good. "We" are all there is. What are the benefits? Well, we would get to rely on our intellect alone because there would be nothing else to rely on. That could be good or bad depending on the results we're experiencing in our lives.

We would be able to take complete credit for all of our great accomplishments. We really wouldn't be accountable to anything higher than us so we would be able to do whatever we pleased as long as we were willing to live with the results of our actions, or as long as we didn't get caught.

Depending on how a person looks at it there could seem to be some possible short-term benefits here.

Downside to Disbelief

So what's the downside to not believing in a higher power for good? No help would be the biggest negative. If we found ourselves with a terminal illness there may be no hope of recovery. End of life story. When life throws us a curve as it often does, we would be left to our own efforts to find our way through. Of course we would always have access to our fellow humans, but they also would have their limits.

Another potential downside is that our lives would likely become more complicated. With human nature being what it is, we could get ourselves into some trouble if we didn't believe we were accountable to some higher authority for our actions. Potential downside does exist if we choose to rely on ourselves alone.

Risk and Reward

There does appear to be several significant benefits to believing in a higher power, with very little risk and no real downside. On the other hand there seems to be little if any benefit to not believing in a higher power and that appears to come with some risk. At the end of this chapter you'll have the opportunity to begin proving to yourself whether there is a higher power for good or not. After all how beneficial is logic and theory without proof.

Left to ourselves we humans don't always do what's best. This is even true of religious people. Throughout history, religions in the name of God have imposed incredible harm and destruction. That's why I make a very clear distinction between the highest power for good and religion.

Self-righteousness, dogmatic statements that are not 100 percent provable, as well as disrespect for other human beings who don't have the same belief, are not characteristics associated with Love (God is Love).

I don't mean to say that all people who follow religion don't display the thoughts and behavior of love; I've just observed that too many fall short. There are also people practicing true religion who are truly real life superheroes. Mother Teresa comes to mind. A true superhero in the eyes of those she served and in the eyes of the world.

Good and Evil

What about the concept of evil and good? Evil, does it exist? It would probably have to. How can the concept of good exist without the concept of evil? Without one, it would be hard to understand the other.

Each one is dependent on the other for its existence. Think of it this way, do positive thoughts and negative thoughts exist? Of course they do. Positive thoughts affect good results and negative thoughts affect bad results.

Negative thinking alone will cause a fair amount of evil to exist in our lives. If we are negative, fault finding, complaining, bitter people, what kind of results are we likely to experience? We humans create enough of our own evil without having to find something else to blame it on. Now there certainly could be an external source of evil beyond what we create, but too often we're not making its job very difficult.

Massive pain and suffering have been caused by those with a negative focused mindset. Hitler focused people's attention on hate and was nearly successful and wiping out an entire race of people.

His twisted philosophy ended his life early and placed his own nation in ruins. How much pain and disillusionment was caused for the surviving Jews? How much pain and disillusionment was caused for the surviving Germans?

Yes, evil does exist and we humans manufacture a lot of it ourselves. Even religious followers have participated in evil acts; the Christian Crusaders went around killing and plundering those who would not follow them. Now that's not a very effective way to get people to follow the religion of love and mercy.

Good also exists as we can clearly see by what happened immediately after the Sept. 11 tragedy in the United States. The following pain and shock affected the entire human race. People quickly jumped into a mode of love, compassion and service.

All differences and disrespectful thinking were set aside. We put our arms around each other and cried together. We worked hard together to take care of the immediate needs. Tragedy brings out the best in us.

Nations around the world stopped in horror and their hearts and prayers went out to the United States. All too soon we forget this beautiful feeling of love. Too bad we don't love each other like this all the time instead of waiting for tragedy.

Yes, good also exists and we each have the choice to manufacture it every day. Compassion, love, understanding, respect and personal responsibility toward each other are the evidence of good. We need to pursue these superhero traits every moment in order to impact ourselves and others in the most positive way. We are free-will-agents and we choose how we think and act. What we choose to think and do affects everything. There's no exception to this rule.

The Need for Higher Power

If we are free-will-agents, and if we are so incredibly intelligent on our own, why don't we do what's best for everyone involved? I would like to suggest that maybe we're not always as bright as we think we are. Oh we're bright all right, just take a look around at all the animals; none can come close to our ability. We just have some big limitations.

When left to ourselves we can be like selfish little children reaping havoc on everyone and causing ourselves a lot of problems. Look at politics in action, for that matter take a peek into any corporate boardroom to see this behavior at its worst.

Superheroes really have no part in self-serving destructive practices. Superhero's have a code to live by and often rely on a higher source of power to help them do what needs to be done.

That's why I like the idea of belief in something greater than us. Something that represents love, selflessness and incredible power for good. If we choose to believe in a higher power for good and we strive to develop a relationship with it, we give a new meaning to the term "having friends in high places". We have a connection to a powerful force for good. A force that can help us reach our highest potential.

Prove it to Yourself

Proof of the existence of this higher force for good is really all we need. There is some logic behind wanting to believe in a higher power. The benefits of believing far outweigh any perceived disadvantages. There really isn't any risk at all. There's only risk if we don't choose to believe in a higher good.

Is it possible for us to test this theory and prove the existence of such an incredible force? Surprisingly, we can. I've already proven it to myself and have been reaping incredible benefits as a result. You can prove it to yourself too, in the privacy of your own life.

The first step is to attempt communication with this higher power for good. Communication is where all relationships start.

What's the easiest and most effective way to communicate with this great power? This is so simple it almost seems silly. But proof is proof and that's what we're after. We will start our communication with the Highest Power in existence by writing it a letter. Don't laugh. And don't worry I won't ask you to actually mail it.

Letters, why letters you ask? Let me ask you this question, why do people find communication over the Internet so attractive? The answer is, you're not face-to-face. You're connected at a distance and that makes it easier to bear your soul. You can share your hopes, deliver bad news, rant and rave and express your deepest feelings much easier if you're not face-to-face with someone on the other end.

This same concept applies to communicating with the highest power in our universe. I can tell you from my own experience that I find this practice to be very effective. When you write, you clarify your thoughts and are able to express yourself more freely. You are focused and involved. It's just a deeper level of communication.

You'll need to have paper and pencil or pen ready. You may also want to find a place where you can store your letters if you're interested in tracking the results.

Keep in mind they should be kept in a place that's very private, where you know no one else will find them. You want to be able to write everything, and I do mean everything without worrying that someone will read what you've written. If you don't care to track your letters or if you're afraid someone may find them, just destroy the letters immediately after you write them. Rip them up, shred them, whatever it takes. They'll still be just as affective, you just won't have a way to track the results.

As you write to your Higher Power try to be like a little child. Communicate what's on your mind and in your heart, honestly and without fear. Don't get all hung up on do's and don'ts. There are no hard fast rules. Just be yourself, your real inner self. Be totally open and honest, anything goes.

Some people have had bad religious experiences because of faulty human beings and they're mad at God. That's okay. You can be mad, you can be sad, you can even shout (on paper) at your higher power. You can ask anything. Pour it all out. Bare your soul. Wright and write till you can't write anymore.

Here's where the proof comes in. Once you're all done breaking the ice in your letter, ask your higher power to help you gain the absolute most you can from this book. Ask for guidance in your life, for wisdom, commonsense and good judgment. Ask for help to eliminate your internal enemies of fear, worry, and doubt. Ask for a clear understanding of what you need to do to reach your highest potential. Ask for the help and intervention you need to achieve it. In your closing, thank your higher power for caring about you and for loving you. Ask to experience the incredible power for good that's available to you.

Sign your name and put the date at the bottom. That's all there is to it. After you complete this book ask yourself this simple question, "did I receive fantastic help from a higher power throughout this material and is my life improving because of it?"

The results you get from writing this letter will provide tangible proof. Put aside your skepticism for now. Don't believe me or anyone else. Write this letter and prove it to yourself. Just be prepared for some very awesome results.

In chapter 10 you'll be shown some additional methods and examples of how to communicate more effectively with your Higher Power. For now just write from the heart and that's enough to get you off to a powerful start.

Points to Remember

- You can choose what you believe.
- If what you believe has the potential to benefit you, believe it.
- Belief in a higher power is not a bad thing and potentially a very good thing.
- There is often a separation between God and religion, don't confuse the two.
- Put it to the test and prove it to yourself.

Just lighten up and have fun with this. Start writing your higher power every day, just short little notes whenever you get a chance. It's actually great therapy and you may be surprised at the benefits you receive.

In the next chapter you'll be discovering the very things that make you incredibly valuable, your unique talents and abilities. Be sure to write a letter to your higher power asking for help to make this the best self-discovery process possible so you can gain the absolute most from the experience. Turn the page and get ready to have some fun discovering the things that make you so great.

U – Unique Value

Chapter 4: "Unique Strengths & Abilities – Discover Your Unique Value And Start Reaping Big Rewards By Benefiting Others!"

You're a Little Different, Good Thing!

You are different from any person who has ever existed, you're also different than anyone who will ever exist in the future and that makes you rare. From the endangered animal to an unusual stone anything that is rare is extremely valuable, including you.

Your imagination, skills, experiences, talents, thoughts and approach to life are different in some way from everyone else's. When you begin to understand the importance of this truth you'll begin to see that you really do have something unique and valuable to offer the world. To the degree you discover and develop your unique capabilities is to the degree you will benefit the world and yourself.

The Value in Strength and Weakness

To begin the journey toward your great potential you'll need to understand exactly what your value is. The value you bring to the world will be the foundation for your success.

You're actually a very complex being made up of a combination of positive productive traits, as well as negative destructive traits.

Every successful business has an understanding of their strengths and weaknesses and so should you. When you're aware of your unique talents and abilities you begin to find opportunities to capitalize on them. When you understand your weaknesses you can be on guard, looking for ways to minimize their destructive impact on your life.

Your weaknesses are the very things that will prevent you from reaching your greatest potential. No matter how much you develop your best qualities, your worst qualities have the potential to destroy everything you gain. Negative traits are the kryptonite of your superhero pursuit. You will need a good understanding of all your traits, good and bad, in order to pursue excellence.

Personality Type Versus Personality Traits

There are a number of personality assessments available to help you understand your personality type. Some models show four basic personality types, others may have 16. Most of these provide reasonable feedback about your personality.

But let's face it, there are literally billions of people in the world and everyone is different. To categorize billions of people into 16 categories seems a bit too general.

I've taken a number of these personality profiles myself and have received some useful information. However I usually find that I have some individual traits that apply to almost every personality type listed. That being said, I decided to take a little different approach for this material.

While developing the personality profile you are about to take, I examined several Psychological approaches to personality profiling, as well as the common Astrological approach to personality profiles. To my amazement there were quite a few parallels between the two approaches.

It seems almost every personality profile, no matter its origin, is comprised of a finite number of individual traits. Each approach just groups the traits together differently. That applies whether you are a Taurus from Astrology, an ENTJ from the Keirsey temperament sorter, or an Otter from Gary Smalley's four animal personality profiles.

Every person has some traits from each personality type. For this program I decided to list all personality traits from each personality type, individually. This way you can rank each individual trait according to how it applies to you, more accurately defining the traits that are you. You won't be limited to some category or personality type that may only have a fair percentage of your traits.

Direction from Higher Power

Before you begin your personal traits analysis I suggest that you take a minute to write a brief note to your Higher Power asking for help to gain great insight and understanding about yourself. The better you understand your strengths and weakness the stronger your foundation for successful living will be.

Seeking a little direction and help from an all-knowing, all-powerful source isn't a bad idea, especially if you want to fulfill your highest potential.

The following is an example of the type of letter you could write to your Higher Power. Keep in mind it's always more powerful and effective to write your own letter in your own words, sincerely, from your own heart. Your letter to your Higher Power may go something like this…

Dear Higher Power,

As you know, I'm trying to find my way in this life. I want to become the very best I possibly can so I can live a fulfilling, productive and meaningful life.

I want to honor you by becoming all that you would have me be. Please inspire me greatly on this exercise and help me to truly understand my strengths and weaknesses, and the unique value I can bring to the world. Help me to put my strengths to better use in service to you and my fellow human beings. Grant me victory over my weaknesses and deliver me from their sting. Help me live up to my incredible potential. Thank you in advance for all your great help, direction, and care.

Love,
Sign Your Name

That's it, you're ready to start. You can copy this letter word for word if you like and it will still help, but it will be even more effective if you put it into your own words. I also find that handwritten notes work best for me. Feel free to try various methods to see what works best for you, in any case, it will work. Just have fun with it.

Your Positive Traits Inventory

In the following pages you'll work through an exercise that's designed to help you discover and quantify your strengths. This is your Positive Traits Inventory.

Read each statement in the assessment that follows then rate how well that statement applies to you personally. The rating scale is a scale from 1 to 10. A rating of 1 would indicate that you are rarely or never like the statement. A rating of 10 would indicate that you are frequently or always like the statement.

The inventory consists of ten categories of statements with ten questions in each category. At the end of each category add up your score and put down your total score for that category.

Once you have completed your inventory, you will simply list your highest scoring individual statements, regardless of the category they are in. Begin with statements scoring a rating of 10, then statements rating 9, 8 and so on.

List as many as you can until you have listed your top 20 positive qualities. When you have completed this inventory you'll be looking at the best of the positive traits you've been blessed with. These are the tools that will help you accomplish your purpose in life.

It's critical to rate each statement as honestly as possible in order to gain a true understanding of your great value. You may want to have a spouse or friend do a separate positive traits inventory for you. Have them rank you as they see you on each of these traits. That way you'll understand how others see you in addition to how you see yourself. Just keep in mind that others will probably see you differently than you see yourself.

Try to keep an open mind and strive to honestly understand your positive traits. Go ahead take a look at the next few pages, take this assessment and begin to realize the incredible value you have to offer.

POSITIVE QUALITIES & STRENGTHS INVENTORY - Page 1

Rating: (Rarely / Never) 1-2-3-4-5-6-7-8-9-10 (Frequently / Always)

The Qualities of Ambition & Originality	Rating
I tend to come up with original ideas.	_____
I enjoy developing creative strategies.	_____
I have courage to move ahead with new things.	_____
I am confident in my abilities.	_____
I have a strong desire to succeed.	_____
I am Independent.	_____
I am self-reliant.	_____
I strive to make progress.	_____
I am innovative.	_____
I love exploring new ideas and solutions.	_____
Total for Ambition & Originality	_____

The Qualities of Cooperation & Diplomacy	Rating
I strive for cooperation when working with others.	_____
I try to encourage harmony when I sense discord.	_____
I have strong interpersonal skills.	_____
I strive to be patient with others.	_____
I have empathy for people who are having difficulty.	_____
I go out of my way to be friendly.	_____
I handle situations with diplomacy.	_____
I strive to understand where people are coming from.	_____
I try to be an open-minded person.	_____
I strive to listen to others when they talk.	_____
Total for Cooperation & Diplomacy	_____

POSITIVE QUALITIES & STRENGTHS INVENTORY - Page 2

Rating: (Rarely / Never) 1-2-3-4-5-6-7-8-9-10 (Frequently / Always)

The Qualities of Inspiration & Expression	Rating
I tend to be spontaneous.	_____
I can be very expressive or animated.	_____
I enjoy entertaining others.	_____
I am enthusiastic.	_____
I have charisma.	_____
I have a strong imagination.	_____
I enjoy being in the spotlight.	_____
I possess creative talent.	_____
I am upbeat about life.	_____
I am passionate when expressing my views.	_____
Total for Inspiration & Expression	_____

The Qualities of Reliability & Hard Work	Rating
I organize my work to be more productive.	_____
I am logical.	_____
I strive to be accurate and precise.	_____
I prefer working with factual information.	_____
I prefer that which is practical and proven.	_____
I am a hard worker.	_____
I am loyal to those I serve.	_____
I believe that honesty is the best policy.	_____
I am reliable.	_____
I am persistent.	_____
Total for Reliability & Hard Work	_____

POSITIVE QUALITIES & STRENGTHS INVENTORY - <u>Page 3</u>

Rating: (Rarely / Never) 1-2-3-4-5-6-7-8-9-10 (Frequently / Always)

<u>The Qualities of Adventure & Independence</u>	<u>Rating</u>
It is important for me to have my freedom.	_____
I love to experience life on the edge.	_____
I enjoy a good challenge.	_____
I thrive on variety and change.	_____
I love learning through experiences.	_____
I delight in new places and situations.	_____
I tend to be a risk taker.	_____
I thrive on adventure.	_____
I love to travel.	_____
I can adapt easily to new situations.	_____
Total for Adventure & Independence	_____

<u>The Qualities of Loyalty & Love</u>	<u>Rating</u>
I have love and concern for others.	_____
I strongly value friendships and family.	_____
I enjoy people.	_____
I strive to reconcile differences between people.	_____
I am nurturing toward those in need.	_____
I feel compassion for people who are suffering.	_____
I am understanding of others shortcomings.	_____
I am loyal to family and friends.	_____
I am fully committed to my relationships.	_____
I put others needs before or equal to my own.	_____
Total for Loyalty & Love	_____

POSITIVE QUALITIES & STRENGTHS INVENTORY - Page 4

Rating: (Rarely / Never) 1-2-3-4-5-6-7-8-9-10 (Frequently / Always)

The Qualities of Investigation & Examination	Rating
I examine things closely.	_____
I easily find inconsistencies.	_____
I enjoy finding the solution to a problem.	_____
I pay attention to the details.	_____
I think things through.	_____
I like to refine things to improve them.	_____
I like to figure things out.	_____
I desire to understand what, when, where and how.	_____
I have a logical approach to examination.	_____
I am a deep thinker.	_____
Total for Investigation & Examination	_____

The Qualities of Leadership & Efficiency	Rating
I am comfortable when in leadership or authority.	_____
I find ways to motivate myself.	_____
I prefer to be in control.	_____
I have the ability to think on my feet.	_____
I strive to accomplish as much as possible.	_____
I don't mind making decisions that impact others.	_____
I have a natural tendency to lead or manage others.	_____
I manage my resources well.	_____
I prefer to have a strategy or plan.	_____
I am very efficient.	_____
Total for Leadership & Efficiency	_____

POSITIVE QUALITIES & STRENGTHS INVENTORY - Page 5

Rating: (Rarely / Never) 1-2-3-4-5-6-7-8-9-10 (Frequently / Always)

The Qualities of Selflessness & Humanitarianism	Rating
I have a desire to care for the needy.	_____
I sympathize with others who are having difficulty.	_____
I tend to be considerate of other's needs.	_____
I believe in showing love and mercy.	_____
I have a strong social conscience.	_____
I am committed to the ideal of universal love.	_____
I strive to show kindness to others.	_____
I strive to perform acts of unselfish service.	_____
I have a desire to help charitable organizations.	_____
I strive to be a generous giver.	_____
Total for Selflessness & Humanitarianism	_____

The Qualities of Insight & Spirituality	Rating
I tend to look at things from a spiritual point of view.	_____
I always seem to be seeking the truth.	_____
I enjoy gaining deep spiritual understanding.	_____
I tend to be Idealistic.	_____
I have faith in a power greater than myself.	_____
I am willing to sacrifice to benefit of others.	_____
I am motivated to live by my beliefs.	_____
I tend to be focused on the spiritual.	_____
I see the best in others.	_____
I like to share spiritual knowledge with others.	_____
Total for Insight & Spirituality	_____

Now that you've identified your positive traits, pick out your greatest strengths and rank them in order of importance to you. On the next page list your three highest scoring categories with the highest score first, second highest next and third highest score last. These three categories will show you the general areas you are strongest in.

Next examine your top strengths individually, regardless of category. List each statement you've ranked with a high score starting with the highest scores at the top of your list. Any statement that ranks a 10 first, followed by the 9's, 8's and so on until you have listed your top 20 positive traits.

MY STRONGEST CATEGORIES

1. _____
2. _____
3. _____

MY TOP 20 STRENGTHS

1. _____
2. _____
3. _____
4. _____
5. _____
6. _____
7. _____
8. _____
9. _____
10. _____
11. _____
12. _____
13. _____
14. _____
15. _____
16. _____
17. _____
18. _____
19. _____
20. _____

Next, list any special abilities or skills you possess below. For example, painting, music, engineering, technical aptitude, public speaking, troubleshooting, writing, gardening… you get the idea.

SPECIAL ABILITIES

_____
_____
_____
_____
_____
_____
_____
_____
_____
_____
_____
_____
_____
_____
_____
_____
_____
_____
_____
_____
_____
_____

As a final step in your positive self-assessment, take a few minutes to examine some of your accomplishments to date. In the space below write down some of the things you've accomplished in your life. Anything you're proud of. If you won a competition, set a goal and accomplished it, or tried your absolute best in some situation.

As you write down each accomplishment try to think about what motivated you to accomplish what you did. How did you feel when you reached your objective? What positive lessons can you learn about yourself from your winning experiences? Write down what you can learn about yourself from your past successes.

PAST SUCCESS AND LESSONS LEARNED

Think About and Use What You've Got

Congratulations, you have just taken the first step toward incredible living. You now have a solid grasp of the positive traits that make you valuable. From now on be on the lookout for opportunities to use your strengths in order to add value to the world around you. Always be ready to spring into action to use your gifts.

Strive to read your top 20 positive traits every morning, noon, and night. Actively look for ways throughout each day to use your abilities to help others, at work, in your home, and in all your activities. As you do you'll begin to feel the superhero emerging from inside of you.

As you begin the next portion of your personal assessment make sure your mind is highly focused on your top 20 strengths while you examine the weaker traits you need to be aware of.

Chapter 5: "Unique Weakness – Know Your Kryptonite So You Can Minimize The Damage It Causes In Your Life!"

The Destructive Power of A Little Weakness

Failure is the result of a weakness uncontrolled. You could have it all, good looks, popularity, connections, money, power and position, but one little weakness can ruin it all very quickly. The only thing your negative traits can bring you is trouble.

Your only chance is to overcome them or at least to minimize their negative effects on your life. But before you can put a damper on their destructive affects you've got to know what your weaknesses are.

Knowledge of Weakness is Power

Please keep in mind that this negative traits assessment is not to be used to depress or discourage you. Every human being has more than a few faults. By taking this negative traits inventory you're just putting yourself in a position to benefit from yours. As you become more aware of your human faults you'll be in a better position to help yourself avoid unnecessary problems.

Superman knew Kryptonite was his weakness so he avoided it like the plague. You also want to avoid the behaviors that can cause your demise.

Every person has negative traits; in fact many of us have a lot of negative traits. That's ok. With a full understanding of both your strengths and your weaknesses, you'll be well ahead of the mediocre masses who are unaware of theirs. And that's exactly where you want to be.

Know Your Top Ten Offenders

It's always best for our mental health to put more focus on the positive rather than the negative. This principal also applies to understanding your unique self. In the previous chapter you focused on identifying your top 20 positive traits.

In this chapter you'll be focusing on identifying your top 10 negative traits. This will help you to stay focused on the positive while allowing you to make progress towards reducing the negative effects of your weaknesses.

At the end of this assessment you'll list the top 10 negative traits that are causing you grief. You'll list them in order with the highest scoring traits at the top of the list, in order of their potential to interfere with your success.

For example, if you rate a 10 on being impractical and a 10 on having difficulty controlling anger, list the anger first. The anger would probably have more potential to negatively impact your life than being impractical would.

Don't fret over the exact placement on the list. Do the best you can and just strive to list your top 10 offenders. That's good enough to make you aware of the negative traits that have the greatest potential to prevent you from fulfilling your purpose.

As soon as you're ready, turn the page to begin uncovering your damaging negative traits and start claiming victory over them.

NEGATIVE TRAITS INVENTORY   Page 1

Rating: (Rarely / Never) 1-2-3-4-5-6-7-8-9-10 (Frequently/Always)

<u>Traits of a Bad Temper</u>   <u>Rating</u>
I tend to have difficulty controlling my temper.   _____
I tend to become resentful.   _____
I tend to be easily angered.   _____
I tend to want revenge.   _____
I tend to become violent when I am angry.   _____
I have a tendency to argue.   _____
I tend to be verbally cruel when I'm angry.   _____
I tend to be irritable when things don't go my way. _____
I tend to be stubborn and closed minded.   _____
When I am angry I tend to speak before I think.   _____

        Total for Traits of a Bad Temper   _____

<u>Traits of Self Belittling & Negativism</u>   <u>Rating</u>
I tend to be overly dependent on others.   _____
I tend to focus on the negative.   _____
I tend to feel inferior to others.   _____
I tend to be jealous of others.   _____
I tend to be over sensitive.   _____
I tend to be pessimistic.   _____
I tend to put myself down.   _____
I tend to be very shy.   _____
I tend to think of others as being better than I am. _____
I tend to focus on why I can't rather than on why I can. _____

        Total for Self Belittling & Negativism _____

NEGATIVE TRAITS INVENTORY   Page 2

Rating: (Rarely / Never) 1-2-3-4-5-6-7-8-9-10 (Frequently/Always)

Traits of Dishonesty & Laziness	Rating
I am inclined to cheat to get ahead.	_____
I tend to be deceptive.	_____
I tend to be dishonest.	_____
I tend to overly exaggerate.	_____
I tend to lie.	_____
I tend to be careless.	_____
I tend to be indifferent.	_____
I tend to be irresponsible.	_____
I tend to be lazy.	_____
I tend to procrastinate.	_____
Total for Dishonesty & Laziness	_____

Traits of Self Importance	Rating
I tend to have a big ego.	_____
I tend to brag.	_____
I tend to make dogmatic statements.	_____
I tend to have excessive pride.	_____
I tend to focus on me.	_____
I tend to be selfish.	_____
I tend to love power.	_____
I tend to be overbearing.	_____
I tend to feel superior to others.	_____
I tend to be vain.	_____
Total for Self Importance	_____

NEGATIVE TRAITS INVENTOR   **Page 3**

Rating: (Rarely / Never) 1-2-3-4-5-6-7-8-9-10 (Frequently/Always)

Traits of being Critical & Ungrateful	Rating
I tend to be cynical.	____
I tend to be critical of others.	____
I tend to focus on others faults.	____
I tend to be impatient.	____
I tend to be intolerant.	____
I tend to be discontent.	____
I tend to complain.	____
I tend to be ungrateful.	____
I tend to take others for granted.	____
I am rarely satisfied with what I have.	____

            Total for being Critical & Ungrateful   ____

Traits of Fear and Mistrust	Rating
I tend to be filled with anxiety.	____
I tend to be a coward.	____
I tend to be fearful.	____
I tend to worry.	____
I tend to be skeptical.	____
I tend to be spineless.	____
I tend to be suspicious.	____
I tend to focus on others negative traits.	____
I tend to speculate about people's motives.	____
I tend to think that the world is against me.	____

            Total for Fear and Mistrust   ____

NEGATIVE TRAITS INVENTORY   Page 4

Rating: (Rarely / Never) 1-2-3-4-5-6-7-8-9-10 (Frequently/Always)

Traits of being Inconsiderate & Interfering	Rating
I tend to be crude.	_____
I tend to gossip.	_____
I tend to be inconsiderate.	_____
I tend to be interfering.	_____
I tend to lack sensitivity.	_____
I tend to meddle in other people's business.	_____
I tend to be degrading towards others.	_____
I tend to be sarcastic.	_____
I tend to be vulgar.	_____
I tend to be rude.	_____
Total for being Inconsiderate & Interfering	_____

Traits of Indecisiveness & Lack of Emotion Control	Rating
I tend to be overly emotional.	_____
I tend to be indecisive.	_____
I tend to lack direction.	_____
I tend to be impractical.	_____
I tend to be Indifferent.	_____
I tend to be inconsistent.	_____
I tend to be moody.	_____
I tend to make poor decisions.	_____
I tend to let my emotions control my thoughts.	_____
I have difficulty keeping my feelings under control.	_____
Total for Indecisiveness & Lack of Emotion Control	_____

NEGATIVE TRAITS INVENTORY   **Page 5**

Rating: (Rarely / Never) 1-2-3-4-5-6-7-8-9-10 (Frequently/Always)

Traits of Self Indulgence & Excess	Rating
I tend to over indulge in alcohol or drugs.	_____
I tend to over indulge my sensual desires.	_____
I tend to over eat.	_____
I tend to be obsessive about weight loss.	_____
I tend to indulge in gambling.	_____
I strive to get what I want regardless of consequences.	_____
I tend to focus on fulfilling my own desires.	_____
I tend to be materialistic.	_____
I tend to be self-centered.	_____
I tend to be obsessive or compulsive.	_____
Total for Self Indulgence & Excess	_____

Evaluate your answers from this exercise and on the next page list your top 10 negative qualities with highest scores first, in order of their ability to negatively impact your life. You just want to capture your main offenders so you can be aware of them.

MY HIGH SCORING NEGATIVE CATEGORIES
1._____
2._____
3._____

MY TOP 10 NEGATIVE HUMAN TRAITS
1._____
2._____
3._____
4._____
5._____
6._____
7._____
8._____
9._____
10._____

Review this list daily along with your strength's list so you can be focused on what you want and don't want in your life. This practice will help you stay positively focused while remaining humble, and that's not a bad thing. Self-examination can be a little painful but it's of incredible value. It gives you a huge advantage over the majority of people who never take stock of themselves.

Profit from Past Failure

Next let's examine some of the failures you've experienced and look for causes. On the next page write down the major failures in your life. As you write them down think about all the things that contributed to each failure.

Although circumstances and other people often play a role in our failures, there's nothing we can do about them. We also play a role in our failures, and we can do something about that.

We can learn from past mistakes. We can be aware of our own negative traits and the consequences they bring. We can change and improve ourselves. Concentrate only on where you have been wrong in order to root out damaging faults that could strike again. Try to list behaviors you've displayed that contributed to any failures or that may have made a situation worse? What are your trouble areas? What can you learn about yourself from past failures?

PAST FAILURES AND LESSONS LEARNED

_____
_____
_____
_____
_____
_____
_____
_____
_____
_____
_____
_____
_____
_____
_____
_____
_____
_____
_____

Congratulations, you now have a grasp of your negative traits so you can begin to catch yourself before you experience too much damage in the future. You can now focus on ways to overcome the traits that have held you back from attaining the life you really want. You can begin to find ways to improve.

Those who never face their faults are doomed to repeat the same mistakes over and over again. Not so for you, now you can seek help and strive to do better from now on.

Get Help Where You Need It

Make a list of people, organizations, programs and books that could help you overcome your negative traits. List any resource you can think of. If any of your negative qualities are causing serious problems in your life with regards to your health, relationships, career, or spiritual growth, get as much help as you can as soon as you can.

Negative traits will waist your valuable time, they steal away the quality of life you could otherwise have. The good news is, none of these negative traits are uncommon to humanity. There's a great deal of experience and help available for the asking. Seek help and you will surely find it.

You now have a genuine picture of who you are today; this is the starting point for becoming the absolute best you can be. The insight you've gained to this point is the cornerstone for incredible advancement.

Now let's put it all together. On the next page, summarize everything you've learned about yourself through this entire self-assessment process.

Self-Assessment In Summary

In Summary My Positive Traits and Talents Are:

_____
_____
_____
_____
_____
_____
_____
_____
_____
_____
_____
_____

In Summary My Negative Traits or Bad Habits are:

_____
_____
_____
_____
_____
_____
_____
_____
_____
_____
_____
_____

I have learned the following lessons about myself:

_____
_____
_____
_____
_____
_____
_____
_____
_____
_____
_____
_____
_____
_____
_____
_____

Remember to review this new understanding of yourself every day so it's fresh in your mind and ready to be put to good use throughout your days.

In the next chapter you'll take the raw materials you've identified in this chapter and build on them. You'll begin to focus them into an incredibly powerful force for positive change. You are a superhero in the making.

Get ready to move on to the next powerful step in the SUPERMAN formula "Passion & Purpose". If you thought this chapter had any value at all, you'll be blown away by the power of the next step.

P - Passion and Purpose

Chapter 6: "Passion & Purpose – Experience Real Personal Fulfillment and Excitement In Living!"

The Transforming Power of Passion

Passion makes you feel alive! When you're filled with passion you beam like a bright shining star and everyone can see it in your face. They feel it when they're in your presence. Just think, if your passion has an effect on others, imagine what it's doing for you.

Passion makes life fun and worthwhile, it's like being in love and that's really what it is. Passion is the love for what you're doing at the moment. With passion turned on you don't have to worry about motivating yourself, you're driven from within.

We all need a passion for something worthwhile in order to enjoy life to the fullest. Enthusiasm positively charges every cell in the body, providing energy and a powerful level of commitment. Passion works so well because it feels good, and it generates good feelings in others. It keeps us going when the going gets tough. Nothing great happens without it.

Think about the Wright Brothers in their pursuit to make the first airplane. Everyone around them thought they were nuts. After all if man were meant to fly he would have been born with wings, right?

The Wright Brothers believed they were going to fly and they were excited about it. I'm sure they had numerous exciting conversations about what it would be like to fly in a machine of their own making. Even when they encountered setbacks, passion kept them on track. Passion is powerful.

When we're busy pursuing something that excites us we accomplish great things. We have what it takes to succeed.

Discovering the passion inside of you is something you simply must do. Not sure if you have a passion? Sure you do. When you were younger you knew what it was. You knew that is, until everyone told you it wasn't possible. It wasn't practical. They told you to give up on it, get your head out of the clouds and join the real world.

I'm sure glad the Wright Brothers, Thomas Edison and Henry Ford didn't give up on their unrealistic pipe dreams. If they had we wouldn't be flying all over the world, we probably wouldn't even be driving as soon, and it would sure get dark at night.

Passion finds a way. So what did you dream about when you were young? Was it really impossible? Impossible as creating the first airplane, the light bulb or the revolutionary process for mass-assembling cars?

Maybe it wasn't just the right passion back then. Well you're older and wiser now and certainly more experienced in life. And now you're armed with some detailed knowledge of your strengths and weaknesses. I'd say there's no better time to explore the passion that's waiting to be realized in you.

Picking a Meaningful Purpose

Discovering a meaningful purpose for your life goes hand-in-hand with passion. Knowing what to pursue gives clarity to life. People sometimes ask me if you can really know what your life purpose is? Why not? What if you actually get to help choose your life purpose?

Which do you think will serve you better, to wander through life without direction or meaning or to pick something worthwhile you can get excited about and then pursuing it?

That's what I thought. You were given the ability to choose what you will do with your life. You can choose the type of work you will do, the people you date, the friends you hang out with and many other things. You can also choose what the purpose of your life will be. Besides if you seek direction and guidance from your Higher Power on this matter, you can't lose. When you seek guidance and help to fulfill your great potential you will certainly receive a lot of powerful help toward choosing a worthwhile purpose.

Fulfilling your highest potential is the goal. Being satisfied that you're living your life to maximum potential. Knowing where you're going and enthusiastically working towards that end. Life is certainly more meaningful with a little direction.

So how can you discover your purpose? It's actually the same way you discover your passion. You will actually discover them both at the same time. Knowing your passion provides clues to finding a worthwhile purpose. On the other hand your purpose must include things you can be passionate about. Passion feeds purpose and purpose feeds passion. Combined together they're like a powerful engine that will propel you forward to the ultimate goal of living the best life possible.

How I Discovered My Passion & Purpose

You are about to learn the process for discovering an exciting passion and a meaningful purpose for your life. Believe me this is exciting stuff. Once you learn this process and begin to use it throughout your life you'll find that you are part of an elite class that few ever experience.

The great thing about this process is that it's repeatable. You see, life is full of changes and so are you. What you find exciting and worthwhile at age 21 will differ greatly from what you find exciting and worthwhile at age 45. Super-living is made up of a series of passionate and purposeful pursuits that you enjoy as you achieve them. You begin by selecting the right pursuit for who you are now.

As you succeed, you change and grow as a person. Once you fulfill a passionate purpose you select the next one that is appropriate for who you are at that time. In this way much of your life will be filled with doing things you enjoy and are excited about and that add to a long list of meaningful, successful, accomplishments.

Listed on the next page is a real life example of this process. As a matter of fact this is the process I used to discover the passion and purpose (inside of me) for writing this book.

On the next few pages you can read through my own example of questions and answers so you have a strong understanding of how the process works. After you're familiar with the questions and the process, you'll be answering the same questions for yourself. In the process you'll discover the first of many worthwhile, passionate, purposes that will transform your life into super living.

For each of the following questions listed below I went back to my youth, as far back as I could remember and gave the answers that I would have given back then.

I then continued to answer each question from different points in my life up to the present. I went from about 5 years old up to 10, from 10 to 15, from 15 to 20 and so on, all the way up to the present time. This gave me a very clear picture of who I really am and of what's really important to me.

It's important to follow this same process as you answer these questions for yourself. The reason it's so important is that this process removes what others have imposed upon you as being important. It identifies the things that are truly important to you at the deepest level. You'll see what I mean as you read through my own example. After you read through my example you'll be answering these questions for yourself.

The Questions I Asked and The Answers I Gave

Question Number 1: What were you doing when you were having the most fun?

My Answers from Youth to Present: Alone, catching bees in a jar. Taking apart the lawn mower. Customizing my bike, creating a design and turning my bike into a chopper. Made a skateboard out of an old broken skate and a board. Exploring new things under the house and down the street. Girls. Dreaming and creating. Ideas. Making up my own projects and working on them.

Having fun. One-on-one conversations. Attention, Making people laugh. Making up songs that conveyed meaning and helped me to express my feeling. Expressing myself. Creative writing. Speech and debate and drama. Freedom. Independence. Accomplishing projects of my own creation. Helping others. Bringing out the best in others. Making peoples day.

NOTE: After answering each question I summarized the essence of my answer to the question:
The summary of my answers to question number 1:

I am having the most fun when I am independent, creating and initiating projects of my own making, expressing ideas, bringing out the best in others and helping others.

Question Number 2: What were you doing when you were having the least fun?

My Answers from Youth to Present: School. Homework. Work assigned by others. Hospitals. Life's cruel lessons. The news. Math. Physical labor. Under others authority.

The summary of my answers to question number 2:
I don't enjoy structure, rules, authority, traditional methods, physical labor, others imposing their agenda's on me, when life seems unfair.

Question Number 3: What are the things that give you energy and get you excited?

My Answers from Youth to Present: Building people up. Making others feel good. Helping others. Public situations. Speaking to a crowd. Learning about fascinating subjects. Explaining ideas. Discovering new understanding. Analyzing things. Gaining new insights. Having a purpose or mission. Entertaining people. Creating pet projects.

The summary of my answers to question number 3:
I gain energy from groups of people, helping others, entertaining, projects of my own creation, learning new things, gaining insight, explaining things to others, having a mission or purpose.

Question Number 4: What do you get excited learning or talking about?
My Answers from Youth to Present: Interesting subject and skills. Projects of my own creation. The human condition. Unexplained phenomena. Research and discoveries. My Higher Power. My personal story. Mind over matter. Speed reading and super learning. Self-help programs. Creative approaches to overcoming. The incredible potential of human beings. Solving problems. Techniques that can help people solve their problems.

The summary of my answers to question number 4:
I get excited talking about specialized skills for increasing human performance, solving problems, overcoming obstacles, personal victories, my story, unconventional methods that make up for weaknesses of conventional methods, Higher Power, unexplained phenomena, projects that benefit others.

Question Number 5: What are your greatest strengths? Use your top 20 strengths list here.

My Answers to Question 5 from Youth to Present: I have a strong desire to succeed. I tend to be innovative. I love exploring new ideas and solutions. I have faith in a power greater than myself. I enjoy developing creative strategies. I strive to make progress. I handle situations with diplomacy.

I can be very expressive or animated. I tend to be passionate when expressing my views. I prefer working with factual information. I tend to be loyal to those I serve. I am persistent. It is important for me to have my freedom. I strongly value friendships and family.

I enjoy finding the answer or solution to a problem. I tend to be a deep thinker. I prefer things to be organized and planned out. I have a strong social conscience. I always seem to be seeking the truth. I like to share spiritual knowledge with others.

The summary of my answers to question number 5:
My greatest strengths are faith in a Higher Power, success consciousness, enjoy developing creative strategies, diplomacy, expressiveness, factual, loyal, persistent, independent, value others, solution focused, thinker, truth seeker, enjoy sharing spiritual knowledge.

Question Number 6: Considering all I have learned about myself, what could I be doing that would fill me with passion and meaningful purpose, and that would provide great value and service to others?

My Answers to Question 6: Learn valuable skills and teach others, Motivational/Inspirational Speaker, Author, Instructor, Inventor of improved methods for personal development, Independent consultant, coaching.

NOTE: Some of the answers I came up with for question number 6 interested me. Some of my answers seemed incredibly far away from where I was at the time. I thought, "These answers are great but how in the world can I get from where I am now to where I really would like to be". "After all I do live in a real world with obligations and commitments", I reasoned. Besides how would I feed my family until I could get to where I wanted to be? The solution was found in the answer to the following question.

Question Number 7: Considering where I am today and my obligations, responsibilities, and current circumstances, what could I be doing that would fill me with passion and meaningful purpose, and that would provide great value and service to others?"

My Answers to Question 7: In my spare time I can develop books and programs that will help others to reach their highest potential by using all the greatest skills and abilities known to man. I could develop a program that would be guided by the Highest Power for good to ensure it is the most powerful and effective it can be. This program could benefit large numbers of people, building them up and helping them to become their absolute best.

Next I simply took the summarized version of each answer to questions 1 through 5 and put them together with the 6th and 7th questions placed last.

- **My greatest strengths are:** Faith in a Higher Power, success conscious, enjoy developing creative strategies, diplomacy, expressiveness, factual, loyal, persistent, independent, value others, solution focused, thinker, truth seeker, enjoy sharing spiritual knowledge.

- **I gain energy from:** groups of people, helping others, entertaining, projects of my own creation, learning new things, gaining insight, explaining things to others, having a mission or purpose.

- **I get excited learning and talking about:** I get excited talking about specialized skills for increasing human performance, solving problems, overcoming obstacles, personal victories, my story, unconventional methods that make up for weaknesses of conventional methods, Higher Power, unexplained phenomena, projects that benefit others.

- **I am having the most fun when I am:** Independent, creative, initiating, projects of my own making, expressing, bringing out the best in others.

- **I don't enjoy:** Structure, rules, authority, traditional methods, physical labor, others imposing their agenda's.

- **I could be doing the following things to fill me with passion and meaningful purpose and to provide great value and service to others:** Learning valuable skills and teaching others, Motivational/Inspirational Speaker, Author, Instructor, Invent an improved method for personal development, be an Independent consultant and coach.

- **Considering where I am today and my current obligations, responsibilities, and current circumstances, I could be doing the following things that would fill me with passion and meaningful purpose, and that would provide great value and service to others:** In my spare time I could develop books and programs that will help others to reach their highest potential using all the greatest skills and abilities known to man. Books and programs that are guided by the Highest Power there is to ensure they are the most powerful and effective they can be. Books and programs that could benefit large numbers of people. Building them up and helping them to become their absolute best.

As a result of my going through this process, you are now enjoying the benefits of the first of my programs mentioned above, in the form of this book. This process uncovered enough passion and purpose for me to identify and complete this Superpowers project. I've had a great deal of fun creating this book and I am confident that many will benefit from it.

Higher Help for Discovering Your Passion and Purpose

Before I started going through this exercise I communicated with my Higher Power to ask for direction guidance and inspiration. I recommend for your benefit that you do too. The best place to start with any important issue is by communicating with your Higher Power.

You can ask for inspiration and guidance to help attain the absolute best outcome as you search for your passion and purpose. The following letter is an example of how you may want to write your own letter to your Higher Power.

Dear Higher Power,

Thank you for all the help you have given me so far in my pursuit of excellence. As you know I'm about to start searching to find a passion and a purpose for my life. I ask for your inspiration and guidance in doing just that.

Please inspire me greatly as I go through the following exercise. Help me to zero in on the most pertinent information and insights that will allow me to clearly understand my greatest passion and a meaningful purpose for my life. Help me attain the highest possible good from this exercise so I can ultimately be of maximum benefit to others, the world, and myself. Help me to attain my highest potential. Thank you again for your kindness, guidance, direction, and for your powerful help.

Love,
Sign your name.

Finding Your Passion & Discovering Your Purpose

There's no time to waist. Start discovering your passion and purpose right now. Before you begin to ask yourself the following questions, take a few minutes to relax your mind and body.

Try to relax as you read each question below, then visualize as far back as you can remember to your youth, and answer each question from that perspective. Relate each question first to the ages between 1 and 5, then between 5 and 10, then 10 to 15 and so on, giving your answers from each time period until you reach the present time.

As you begin to remember things, write down whatever comes to mind even if it seems silly at first. First impressions are usually the best indicators of your true self. Just enjoy the exercise and have fun with it. You might be a little amazed at the things you come up with. Are you ready? Here you go!

7 Questions To Find Your Life Purpose

1. What were you doing when you were having the most fun?
   Answer completely then summarize your answers.

2. What were you doing when you were having the least fun?
   Answer completely then summarize your answers.

3. What are the things that give you energy and get you excited?
   Answer completely then summarize your answers.

4. What do you get excited learning or talking about?
   Answer completely then summarize your answers.

5. What are your greatest strengths?
   List your Top 20 strengths from Chapter 5.

6. Considering all I have learned about myself, what could I be doing that would fill me with passion and meaningful purpose and that would provide great value and service to others?
   Write whatever comes to mind.

7. Considering where I am today and my current obligations, responsibilities, and current circumstances, what could I be doing that would fill me with passion and meaningful purpose, and that would provide great value and service to others?"
   Write whatever comes to mind.

When you have answered all of the questions above, take a moment to read through all of your answers. You should start to see a pattern pointing you in some direction. Review my own example again to help you understand how to organize your answers.

Don't put a lot of pressure on yourself and don't worry if you don't seem to get a clear picture right away. Many will find profound answers very quickly, for others it may take a few days. Not a problem. You're moving in the right direction. If you don't get a lot of clarity right away, try the following.

Read your list of summarized answers before you go to bed every night for the next 7 nights. Ask yourself the 6th and 7th questions before you go to sleep. The answers will come. Don't be surprised if you wake up with some exciting insights.

Once you've received answers to the questions listed above you'll have found a purpose you can really get passionate about. Remember this is your first of many valuable purposes. Once you fulfill one purpose you'll need to reevaluate to find your next exciting objective.

Writing this book has been a wonderful passion and purpose for my life, but now it's finished. I'm already on to the next exciting passion. Get a few of these under your belt and you've got some real superhuman accomplishments. Isn't this a lot more exciting than the things you were thinking about a few short days ago?

Your Ultimate Self Portrait - The Rest of Your Story

Now let's finish this section by defining what you ultimately want to be in this life. No doubt you will find great passion and purpose in many projects along your life journey, but you will also want to have an ultimate destination in mind. When you have a picture in your mind of who and what you ultimately want to be, you set the foundation and the tone for a number of important pursuits in your life.

As you develop a clear picture in your mind of the ultimate you, your mind will go to work to help you fulfill that image. You'll begin to choose objectives that support the fulfilling of the ultimate you.

Many of the circumstances and opportunities you begin to encounter will seem to be in support of the ultimate you. You'll start enjoying your life more by pursuing purposeful objectives you're excited about and that will culminate in fulfilling your greatest potential.

Do the following exercises to help you picture the ultimate you.

- List the things you want to be remembered for after you are gone.
- List how you want your spouse, children, parents, and or your friends to remember you.
- List how you want to be remembered at your place of work.
- List the noble causes you want to be associated with.

Finally, write a short story of how you want your life to be from this point on. Imagine that you get to pick how your life will be from now until the end of your days. What would the most ideal life you can imagine be like? Paint a perfect picture of how you want your life to be. Dream big, make it a masterpiece.

What's the point in writing your ultimate Life story? Energy follows attention. When you begin to believe in the possibilities, begin to dream big and forget about limitations, you will set your course for incredible living. Go ahead write the rest of your story and make it a great one.

Onward and Upward

You've come a long way in only a few days. In fact you're well on your way to being a real superhero. You've got a new direction in life.

You understand your unique value and you know what you can do to provide value to others. You're well on your way and far ahead of the majority of your mortal counterparts. Life is becoming exciting, meaningful, and more worthwhile.

Review often everything you've written in this exercise. Keep the images of what you desire alive in your mind. As you do your power of belief will grow. As your belief grows your accomplishments will too.

Remember the old saying "whatever a man can conceive and believe, he can achieve." You'd better believe it!

You've built a great foundation in this and previous chapters. Now you're fully prepared to move towards your true heart's desire. In the next section you'll be gaining incredible expertise in the superpower skills that will help you achieve success in your great pursuits of life.

E – Expertise of Superpowers

Chapter 7: "Expertise Of Mind Over Matter – Master The Power Of A Focused Mind So You Can Affect Positive Results In All Areas of Life!"

"Formulate and stamp indelibly on your mind a mental picture of yourself as succeeding. Hold this picture tenaciously and never permit it to fade. Your mind will seek to develop this picture!" - Dr. Norman Vincent Peale 1898-1993, Author of "The Power of Positive Thinking"

Mind Over Matter – Make Good Things Happen

In Chapter 3 we learned that Scientist have concluded that matter is not solid; it's actually made up of patterns of living energy. Mind over matter simply refers to the ability to affect matter (patterns of living energy) with thought.

As mentioned earlier, the great Nazarene, after healing people would often say, "Your faith has made you well." This statement suggests that human thoughts had something to do with any healing that took place.

Once, while taking a stroll on the water the Nazarene was asked by Peter if he (Peter) could walk on the water to meet him (Jesus). The Master said, come on over. Peter (the human) actually walked on the water. But he looked down and let fear and doubt take over. He began to sink. The Master said, "Oh Peter why did you disbelieve?"

In another reported incident the Master could not perform miracles in his hometown because the people didn't believe. These examples indicate that what we believe or don't believe can actually limit the ability of a Higher Power to help us?

If we believe a Higher Power can help us, it can and will help us. If we don't believe that a Higher Power can help us, it not only won't help us, it can't help us. What we believe in the depths of our hearts and minds plays a role in being able to affect the elements of matter. Or in other words the world around us.

After studying this subject in some depth I am convinced of the power of our thoughts to affect matter. I am also convinced that all people are equipped with this ability. The placebo affect proves this point. People across multiple religions as well as people of no religion have been healed of illness by taking a placebo.

The only common factor in these healings was that these people believed they would be healed and they were. Don't get me wrong, I strongly believe there's a much greater power for good than we humans have typically tapped into. I believe it's critical for us to be guided and directed by the Highest Power there is, especially if we want to fulfill our great potential. But even apart from a Higher Power, the capabilities of our human minds are nothing less than incredible.

These abilities by themselves are neither bad nor good just as a gun is neither bad nor good. It's the way we use the tool that determines whether it is bad or good. We human beings have been created with the ability to affect things with our thoughts. It's an incredible privilege and a huge responsibility we need to respect and use wisely.

The reality of the power of mind over matter is well documented. Martial arts experts, fire-walkers and energy healers all have used the power of their minds to accomplish amazing things even in current times.

Athletes focus the power of their minds to accomplish incredible feats as well. Just try a quadruple jump on ice skates some time without landing on your butt. Heck, try a single. Just standing up on skates can be a challenge for some of us. What about running a sub four-minute mile? Have you done one of those lately? Ever since Roger Banister broke that first 4 minute mile mark, people have been doing it ever since. Yes we do have incredible ability if we choose to use it.

I once saw a TV show about an incredible painter who painted magnificent beautiful paintings. An impressive human ability all by itself. What made this story so fascinating was that the painter was a young woman paralyzed from the neck down. She painted with her teeth.

Her paintings were much nicer than many artists with full use of their limbs. This wasn't modern art either. Trees looked like trees, people looked like people and so on. You could never have imagined that these beautiful works of art were created without hands. Does mind over matter really exist? If that's not focusing your mind to do the impossible I don't know what is. What we believe we can or cannot do greatly affects what we actually do.

Scientific Evidence of Mind Over Matter

In the book "Mind Over Matter" by Loyd Auerbach, the author describes a number of mind over matter experiments conducted in the 60's and 70's by Soviet and US Scientist. Nina Kulagina, also known as Nelya Mikhailova was a very gifted psychic who was studied by both Russian scientists and American researchers J.G. Pratt and Montegue Ullman. Nina was reported to affect movement in a number of objects by using her mind alone.

She was able to cause objects to move, rotate and even rise into the air with the focus of thought.

Another mind over matter phenomena observed in the '70s was metal bending. Uri Geller an Israeli entertainer and psychic was able to bend spoons and other things with his mind.

During the 1980s an aerospace engineer from Southern California named Jack Houch ran a series of metal bending parties conducted at the John F. Kennedy University in the San Francisco Bay area.

During these experiments a number of impressive results were accomplished by groups of ordinary people who had an interest in learning this skill. Some of the results included the bending of forks, spoons, as well as thick metal bars that would have been impossible to bend by human strength alone. How could this be accomplished?

As explained in an earlier chapter, everything is made up of pulsating vibrating energy. Everything produces energy frequency waves. Our thoughts also produce energy thought waves.

When our thoughts are focused and fully charged with emotion, they radiated out from us and actually collide with and have an effect on other energy patterns (other matter). At the very least this ability is nothing less than amazing. So how can the average person use their mind to affect positive results in everyday life?

Mind Over Matter and The Miracle Golf Game

Visualization has been a popular method used for helping people to achieve a desired result. It is actually a form of mind over matter. When you create thoughts of how you want to perform and vividly experience those thoughts as real, you are creating a template for your desired result.

For example, when a person intensely visualizes the successful outcome of giving a speech, they usually have a successful speech. The mind prepares the body to perform at its best. People who are naturally poor speakers often discover that this technique works wonders.

With visualization, the mind is controlling how you perform, altering your normal performance and changing it into a better performance. In other words, your mind can help you do what you are normally incapable of doing. That's a form of mind over matter. Let me share with you one of my own experiences using this form of mind over matter.

I love the game of golf but I'm a terrible golfer. I average a couple of outings per year and usually shoot in the 58 to 64 range for just nine holes. I told you I was bad.

You can't really expect to improve much by playing only a couple of times per year. Or can you? A few years ago I planned to go golfing with my father-in-law on a course in South Dakota. Yes there is a golf course in South Dakota. There's actually more than one. This one is in Scotland South Dakota. I had only picked up a club once in two years and was looking forward to golfing.

However I had a problem, I didn't want to get frustrated by playing a terrible game since I hadn't played in so long. It would have taken all the fun out of the experience. I decided to try a little mind over matter experiment.

Two nights before the game while I was going to sleep, I decided to visualize the whole game in advance. Not just visualize it, but to experience the entire game in great detail. I felt the feelings, saw the scenes and even smelled the grass and trees, all in my mind. I asked myself to feel what it would be like to hit a perfect shot. I saw and experienced perfect shots for every last hole on the course, all in my mind.

It was great fun imagining and experiencing it as if it were real. It was truly the best game I've ever experienced even though it was just imaginary. I told myself this was how I wanted to play on the appointed day.

Well, the appointed day came and I didn't shoot a perfect game. I did however shoot a 46, my best game ever. On one par three I was only a few feet away from a hole in one. I was more than happy to pick up a birdie. I shot the best round of my life and the only thing I did different before this game was to use my mind to prepare myself to do the best I could possibly do.

For me to shoot a 46 on nine holes was a miracle. Especially after only picking up the clubs once in the previous two years and considering my average score was between 58 and 64. My best score before that exciting day had been a 52 and that was during a year when I actually played a number of times. Do I believe in the power of mind over matter? You know I do.

Practical Applications for Mind Over Matter

Energy healers use the power of mind over matter to help heal the sick. Athletes use this power to excel. Unknowing placebo takers use mind over matter to promote healing in themselves. You can use this power to accomplish incredible things too.

You've been given a mind that separates you from all creatures on the earth. You possess free will, and you can choose what you will think and what you will do. It's time to take control of your powerful mind and begin to use it for the benefit of others and yourself. As you learn to combine your incredible human abilities with guidance and help from the Highest Power in the universe, you most certainly will accomplish amazing things.

The simplest and most practical use for mind over matter is to use emotionalized visualization and positive thought focus to influence events in your daily life. Like in the example of my miracle golf game.

A great way to begin practicing this is to visualize yourself in the upcoming day. Do this before falling asleep each evening. Fully experience yourself performing at your best in everything you plan to do the next day. Try the following exercise for 7 days and see what kind of results you get.

Visualization Exercise

Before falling asleep, relax your body and take slow, full, deep breaths. Count backwards from 10 down to the number 1. Relax the muscles in your head, face, neck, arms, body, legs, and feet. When you are fully relaxed, imagine yourself in a favorite place, sitting on a beach or walking through a beautiful forest.

As you begin to feel very comfortable and relaxed in this wonderful place, imagine looking upward and seeing yourself on a large screen. See yourself on the screen getting up from your bed on the following day. See yourself experiencing the next day as you deeply desire it to be.

See yourself in your home, at your work and in all social situations being at your absolute best. See, smell, feel, hear and fully experience everything as if it were real. Experience yourself responding and performing at your absolute best in every situation.

Make it as real as you can. Feel a strong desire within yourself to have this actually become a reality. Have fun with your imagination, enjoy the process and keep a smile on your face as you create this perfect day. Bask in it fully. Stay in this state until you truly believe the experience can actually happen.

Then let go completely and be completely willing to accept whatever happens. Know in your heart that the more often you practice this exercise, more and more positive results will materialize in your life.

At all times strive to keep your desires free of selfishness. Strive to be the best person you can imagine whenever you do this exercise, always have the best interest of everyone in mind. If your desires are pure and in the best interest of everyone involved, good things will happen.

Your mind will powerfully affect your life for the better if you will only take control of it and continuously focus it on the results you want.

Advanced Mind Over Matter

If you're the daring type you may be wondering what else you can do with your powerful mind. Perhaps your thinking "I wonder if I could actually move an object with my mind." Surprisingly a good percentage of people who try the following experiment will actually succeed at moving a light object with thought alone.

I've included this advanced mind over matter experiment that you can do in the privacy of your own home. This experiment is adapted from an experiment described in the book "Mind Over Matter" by Loyd Auerbach.

Before you try this experiment it's time to write a letter to your Higher Power to ensure that you get the most out of this exercise. Fear, doubt and misunderstanding won't help. They will only ensure failure.

Always start something new by seeking a little help and direction from the Highest Power there is. Here's an example…

Dear Higher Power,

I am about to try an experiment to test the ability of mind over matter for myself. I am human and I don't fully understand this stuff but it does seem possible we were created with this ability. If this is true, please help me to prove it to myself convincingly.

I ask you to remove my fears, doubts, and misunderstanding, so I can have the cleanest shot at making this work. If this is ok with you, I ask you to grant me great success in this experiment. I also ask you to help me understand the best possible use of this ability. If this gift can help increase my communication with you, help me to develop it for that purpose as well. Please inspire me and protect me as I try this experiment.

Thank you for your great wisdom, guidance, protection and help in all these things.

Love,
Sign Your Name.

Advanced Mind Over Matter Experiment

Try this experiment at least 21 times in order to increase your chances of success. The first thing you'll need to do is create a very light object that you can attempt to move with your thought waves.

Take a three-inch by three–inch, square piece of paper, grab two opposite corners and fold them together to the shape of a triangle. Unfold it back to the square and fold the other two corners into a triangle.

The goal is to make the piece of paper into a pyramid shape with a high point in the center. This may sound a little strange but take the piece of paper and hold it to your forehead for a few moments, one minute should be long enough. This is to help connect the energy that radiates from your thoughts to the energy (matter) that the paper is made up of.

Next take a needle and insert the thick end into a bar of soap or some other object you can use as a base, let the point of the needle stick straight up in the air. Now, balance your piece of paper or pyramid on the top of the needle. Just rest it gently on top of the needle with the point at the top center of the pyramid resting lightly on the needle. Move the paper with your finger or lightly blow on it to insure that it moves easily. Look at the pictures below to get an idea of how this should look:

Now for the experiment. Relax, close your eyes and count slowly backwards in your mind from ten down to one. Take a deep breath and exhale with each number you count. With each breath relax all the muscles in your body from the top of your head to the bottom of your feet.

Once you are totally relaxed, with eyes closed and pointed slightly upward, visualize yourself concentrating on the piece of paper. See yourself sending out powerful energy waves from your forehead, throat and chest that push the paper making it move, twitch, bob and turn.

Feel the powerful vibrations radiating out from you and pushing the paper. Smile as you feel the excitement of your success. Experience the waves of energy building up, gathering strength and pushing out from you gaining more and more power. Say in your mind, "I can move matter it's only energy, I can move matter it's only energy, I can move matter it's only energy, it's easy and its fun". Repeat this over and over in your mind while in this state, until you feel confident.

Open your eyes and stare at the paper with great intensity. Tense up the muscles in your body as you stare at the paper, feel the deep desire to move the paper with your thoughts and feelings. Focus hard on the paper with all your might.

In your mind firmly tell the paper to "move, move, move", over and over again. Keep up the intensity until you begin to tire. Then quickly relax. Completely relax. Look away from the object for a few moments and start to concentrate your attention on something else for a few moments.

Now turn your head back to the paper. Completely relax, stare at the paper and repeat in your mind over and over again "move, move, move," at least 21 times.

Many of you will actually see the paper move, twitch or bob on your first try. It will probably freak you out at first. The enormity of this discovery will take a little bit to digest. If you don't succeed on the first try just keep trying as often as you can until it moves. Keep this little pin-balancing pyramid near where you focus a lot of mental energy. Like at your desk or by your computer. Chances are very good that with enough practice; you'll see this material object move.

Your thoughts really do affect the things around you. You've always had this ability and it's had both positive and negative effects on you throughout your entire life. You now understand how powerful your thoughts really are. You also understand how important what you think and believe is. From this point on you can begin to focus your powerful mind on affecting the positive results you want.

What You Really Believe is Affecting You

Auto pilot thinking has got to be a concern at this point. What I mean is, we all have a subconscious mind that's busy working in the background all the time. It even works while we sleep. The subconscious mind is powerful and it's working 24 hours a day producing and broadcasting thought waves. So, what's your subconscious thinking about and how is it affecting you?

Have you ever said to yourself, "I know I'm going to fail this test" or "I know I won't make this shot?" The subconscious goes to work to make sure you screw up and you do.

Fortunately, when you really believe you're going to pass that test or make that difficult shot the subconscious will often help you do that too. It usually depends on whether you really believe you can do it or not. The slightest bit of doubt will sink you, kind of like the Apostle Peter walking on the water.

Belief is the key. "The prayer made in faith heals the sick." Ever hear that one before? If you believe completely, without doubt, not even a tiny bit of doubt, big things can happen. On the other hand even a little bit of doubt can have a negative effect.

Belief without doubt seems to be the key. Ask your Higher Power to help you overcome your fears and doubts and a whole new world of possibilities will open up to you. Start believing in the good that can take place in your life. Constantly focus your mind on positive things and stay clear of negative thinking, never lose faith. Know for certain that when the time is right, as long as you believe, great things will happen for you.

Now that you have a good handle on the incredible superpower of your mind to affect your world, turn to the next chapter and begin to attain greater expertise in your super-skill of Intuition!

Chapter 8: "Expertise Of Intuition – Develop The Ability To Use Your Intuition To Make Better Decisions And To Heed Internal Warnings!"

"The intellect has little to do on the road to discovery. There comes a leap in consciousness, call it intuition or what you will, and the solution comes to you, and you don't know how or why."

Albert Einstein

Getting To Know Your Sixth Sense

Gut feelings are common to all of us. We've all felt things we can't really explain through the normal five senses. Perhaps we've met someone for the first time and something didn't feel just right even though this person seemed nice enough on the surface. Later on we may have discovered this person was less than desirable.

Or perhaps we've had a feeling something bad was about to happen, and it did. We all receive good and bad vibes about people, places and situations. In a word it's called intuition. A sixth sense if you will. People with a very strong sixth sense are referred to as being psychic. Indeed some people do have a stronger intuition than others, however the fact remains that we all have this ability to some degree.

Let's take a look at some situations that are considered to be intuitive or psychic. The following descriptions provide some examples of what intuition is. Intuition includes but is not limited to the following descriptions:

- Experiencing a sudden revelation from out of the blue
- Dreams that seem to provide some message or meaning
- Knowing what another person is thinking before they express it
- Thinking of someone before they call or before you run into them
- Sensing things are okay even when everyone else is in turmoil
- Sensing something is wrong even when all outside appearances seem okay
- Sensing good or bad vibrations about people places and things
- Internal warnings or suspicions of impending danger

Intuition is the telepathic ability of receiving information through means other than the normal five senses of sight, sound, hearing, touch, or taste.

Intuition - What Is It Good For – Absolutely Something

Just think how helpful it would be to have a highly developed sixth sense. For example, let's say you're preparing for a meeting with the boss tomorrow and for some reason you're not feeling good about it. You're getting bad vibes about the whole thing.

With this advanced warning you could try a little mind over matter thinking combined with a note to your Higher Power asking for help. Your sixth sense may be giving you advanced warning and you've really got nothing to lose by trying to help the situation. The alternative is to lay awake all night worrying about it, and that definitely won't help. Since you probably wouldn't be able to sleep anyway you may as well give it a shot. Let's briefly follow through on this example to help build upon what was covered in the last chapter on Mind over Matter.

In this example, before going to sleep the night before your meeting with your boss, you could simply ask yourself what you are sensing about this meeting. Maybe you suspect it's about your quota, a recent mistake, or about some negative company news.

Before going to sleep you could write a letter to your Higher Power expressing your concerns and fears and asking for deliverance from anything negative. You could ask for the will of your Higher Power and for things to turn out in the best interest of everyone involved.

Before falling asleep you could experience the meeting in your mind the way you want it to be. Imagine feeling good vibrations, enjoying the conversation. See yourself being a tremendous help to your boss and actually getting some benefit out of the meeting. See your fears as a false alarm, this experience is actually for your good and works out to your great benefit.

Go to sleep accepting that whatever happens will ultimately be for your benefit and for the benefit of everyone involved. The next day, the meeting may turn out to be totally different than you had originally feared. It could actually be very positive. You may receive a new opportunity, a promotion, or some positive recognition.

Of course it doesn't always work this way but you'd be amazed how often things really do work out to your advantage when you focus your thoughts in this way. One thing's for sure, the positive focus of your mind will always yield better results than fear or worry.

Tuning-In To Intuition

Learning to tune-in to what your gut is telling you is the key to receiving intuitive information. And just how does a person do that, you may ask? As with anything it takes practice.

For starters you can begin taking your gut feel temperature throughout the day, especially during situations where you feel a little uncomfortable. When you meet someone, go somewhere, or when you're sitting in a meeting, just relax, slowdown, and mentally step back from what's going on. You're still consciously aware of what's going on of course but you can detach slightly.

Become an observer of your intuitive senses. Ask yourself, in your mind (if you do it out loud people will look at you funny), what am I feeling about this situation and what am I sensing here? What are the core issues beyond surface appearances? Why do I feel this way?

Relax and be patient, very shortly intuitive answers will begin to pop into your head. When you sense that you understand the real essence of what's happening in a given situation. Ask yourself, what can I do to be of value in this situation? Listen for answers.

If you're inspired with a positive answer or a solution that will help solve the problem and that won't cause harm or an offense, then go for it.

Speak up and share your ideas. If you sense it's better to say nothing, or if you keep getting blocked from sharing your insights, then say nothing. It may not be the right time. Learn what you can from your intuitive feelings.

Good and bad vibrations are constantly happening all around you. The more often you practice tuning-in and listening to your gut feelings the more useful your intuition becomes.

Meditation the Intuition Builder

Meditation may be good for your health and well-being but it's also a powerful tool for developing the ability of listening to your gut feelings. It slows down brain waves, relaxes the body, quiet's internal noise and opens you up to the small clear voice inside. Meditation help's tune-out the exterior world and makes you more sensitive to receiving intuitive information.

Meditation is merely the act of tuning-in to deeper subconscious levels of mind. In the normal state of being awake the human brain waves operate between 14 and 30 cycles per second. These are known as Beta brain waves.

As you relax, the next deeper state of awareness is known as Alpha, with brain waves in the 8 to 13 cycles per second range. This is a good state of mind for accelerated learning and for accessing intuitive feelings.

Theta is the next deeper state of relaxation. In this state brain waves slow to the rate of 4 to 7 cycles per second. This is the state where your subconscious solves problems for you while your conscious mind is asleep.

The final state of relaxation is known as Delta. In this state brain waves are at .5 to 3.5 cycles per second. This is the state of deep sleep.

There are a good many relaxation and meditation audios available that can help you achieve a deeply relaxed state of being. These audios are available at almost any bookstore. You'll probably want to try different methods of relaxation until you find what works best for you. I've included a mediation exercise below that can help you get started. It's all about becoming deeply relaxed and giving your mind a time out. It's actually very enjoyable.

Read the following meditation exercise several times before you give it a try. As you read it try to remember the general sequence of events and imagine seeing and feeling all the things that are described. When you feel you've got it, close your eyes and proceed through the exercise to the best of your memory.

Improvisation is OK as long as you can get to a deeply relaxed state of mind. This meditation exercise can also be recorded for playback or read to you by a friend in order to help you enter a deeply relaxed, meditative state. Be sure to read it in a way that is soft and deliberate to help promote relaxation. Once you've tried this exercise a few times you'll be able to do it on your own very easily.

Meditation Exercise

Find a quiet place and make yourself comfortable either sitting up in a chair or lying down with your arms and legs uncrossed. Relax and begin to slowly count backwards from 10 down to the number 1. For each count, take a slow deep breath and exhale completely.

As you exhale, completely relax your body from the top of your head to the bottom of your feet. Totally relax every muscle in your body with each count. Release all thoughts from your mind. Just concentrate fully on your breathing and on completely relaxing your body. Relax deeper and deeper with each count all the way down to the count of 1.

When you have reached the count of 1, imagine you are standing at the top of a large staircase with 10 steps leading down to a beautiful field. Slowly and deliberately walk down each step from 10 all the way down to 1. Feel yourself going deeper and deeper into a relaxed state of mind. Feel your body becoming more and more relaxed with each step. Go deeper and deeper into a wonderful relaxed state of well-being. You feel very good.

As you reach the bottom of the staircase you will be in a beautiful field. You can see the blue sky and the clouds floating by. You smell the grass and the trees, and the river nearby. You hear the sound of birds and the flow of water. Feel the fresh grass under your feet. Feel the gentle breeze on your face and skin.

You are deeply relaxed in this beautiful place. You feel wonderful. You feel so fine. Better than you've felt for such a long time. Off to your left you see something curious in the distance. You notice seven brightly colored doors out in the field. You begin to notice these doors from left to right. As you look at each door you feel more and more peaceful and relaxed. You feel great. Better than ever before. Completely relaxed.

The first door you see is a bright red colored door. The color and texture is like a delicious red apple. You see the perfect red color in your mind. Just to the right of the red door, the second door is the color and texture of an orange. You see the perfect orange color in your mind. You even smell the scent of a freshly cut orange. As you look upon this door it causes you to relax even deeper.

The next door to the right is a bright yellow door. It reminds you of the color of a sour lemon. You can taste the bitter taste of lemon in your mouth. The 4th door, just to the right is lime green and has the texture of a lime. You pause to look at this door and reach out and touch it with your hand. You can feel the lime texture with your hand. Feel the texture, see the green lime color.

The next door to the right is the 5th door. It is a beautiful brilliant blue color that fluctuates between the soft blue sky and a powerful royal blue. It looks so soft, so soothing. As you look at this door you relax even deeper, deeper than before. With each breath you exhale you relax even deeper.

You now see that there are two final doors, the 6th and 7th doors. The sixth door is a brilliant violet color. It is beautiful, pulsating and vibrant. You notice that this door is connected to the seventh door. They are a connected pair of double doors, leading into a special room.

The seventh door is a brilliant pure white light. The most brilliant pure white light you have ever seen. It is so beautiful and peaceful to look at, it makes you feel so warm and good inside. As you look upon these final doors you feel so relaxed, so peaceful and safe. You love the way you feel at this moment. You are at peace and at one with all that is good and pure.

In your mind, see yourself walking over to the six and seventh doors and open them. As you walk through the doorway into the wonderful room, you feel so peaceful, safe and content. The mixture of violet and pure white lights envelope you and fill you with the most beautiful sense of peace you have ever known. You feel wonderful, you feel safe and free. You are more relaxed than ever before.

With each breath you take you feel more and more relaxed. Now, as you sit on the floor of this wonderful place, take three slow deep breaths. Exhale slowly, relaxing completely from the top of your head to the bottom of your feet.

In this state you are completely in-tune with your intuition. You are finely tuned with your sixth sense. Whenever you are in this state, you receive clear intuitive signals and you are able to interpret them with accuracy. Every time you enter this wonderful state of relaxation you become more in-tune with your intuitive ability.

Whenever you ask a question while you are in this relaxed state, you sense accurate flashes of intuitive information and you interpret the information with increasing accuracy. It is fun and exciting to tune-in to your intuitive abilities. You feel so wonderful, so safe, and so at peace.

You sense that the Highest Power in the Universe is with you and you know the communication channels are completely open between you and your Higher Power. All blockages have been removed. You communicate powerfully with your Higher Power in this wonderful state. You feel that you are loved and you know that all wrongs have been forgiven and are remembered no more. In this state there are no problems and no pain.

There is only peace, love, and joy. You feel so safe protected and loved. You know you can ask any question you desire. Simply ask what you desire to know, let your mind be still, and wait. Intuitive answers will come. In this state ask your Higher Power to guide and direct you in His ways and to protect you from harm. Ask for wisdom, common sense, and good judgment. Ask for discernment to know what is good and right. Enjoy the peace fully. Remain in this relaxed state as long as you wish.

While in your relaxed state practice the following exercises to build your intuitive powers: Mentally project yourself into a familiar room, your living room, office, or any other place you are familiar with. In your mind see the objects in the room as vividly as you can. See colors, textures and shapes. In your mind smell the smells of this room, smell wood, glass, metal, plaster, and flowers, anything that is in the room.

Next, in your mind feel the textures and surfaces of objects in the room, a rug, a vase, furniture, lights, anything and everything. Finally, mentally project yourself into various objects in the room. Imagine what it looks like from inside an object, what does it feel like, what does it sound like inside these different objects. Is it dark, light, dense or soft, smooth or rough? What does it smell like? Use your wonderful imagination to fully experience these things, and as you do your intuitive senses will be increased.

After you have successfully projected yourself into rooms and objects, try a mental journey outside and project yourself into plants, trees, fruit, rocks, signs, concrete, the ground, and whatever else your imagination can think of. These exercises will help you tune-in with the things (matter or patterns of living energy) all around you, increasing the sensitivity of your intuitive sensing. Enjoy these exercises; experience these things as fully as you can.

When you're ready to return to your normal sate of awareness, simply count up slowly from 1 to 5. Feel yourself returning to your normal state of awareness, a little more with each count. At the count of 5 stretch your arms and open your eyes feeling wide awake, refreshed and renewed.

Build an Anchor to Return Quickly

After you've reached this deep state of meditation several times you can return to this state very quickly by using what's known as an anchor. Here's how it works. Every time you enter a deep state of relaxation, lightly press your pinky and ring finger of either hand to the palm of the same hand. Then say to yourself, "Anytime I wish to enter this beautiful relaxed state, I will do so as soon as I press my pinky and ring finger against my palm in this manner. Repeat this phrase 3 times and release these two fingers from your palm.

Do this every time you meditate for the first seven times and you will have built a response between your brain and your anchor. After that, whenever you want to relax deeply, just press your pinky and your ring finger of either hand to the palm of the same hand, close your eyes, relax your body from head to toe, and count backwards from 10 down to 1. At the count of 1 you will then be in your deep state of relaxed mediation.

If you've meditated before feel free to use any technique you're comfortable with. You may want to try this exercise at least once, and then just use whatever works best for you.

Practice this meditation exercise as often as you can. Be sure to build your anchor every time so you can achieve this state quickly whenever you desire. Being able to achieve a deep meditative state is key to enhancing intuitive ability. Being proficient at quieting the mind enhances the ability to listen to the still small voice inside.

Advanced Sixth Sense

Remote viewing is a psychic ability that's a little more developed than your average intuition. In the book "Mind Trek" by Joseph McMoneagle, the author discusses in great detail, government experiments that have taken place in an attempt to view targets (remote locations and objects) with psychic ability. The results are nothing less than amazing. Another book, "Miracles of Mind" by Russell Targ a retired senior staff scientist for Lockheed Missile and Jane Katra a PHD, confirms these government experiments and their successes.

There is no doubt that psychic ability exists in people. Based on years of research and personal experience, both Russell Targ and Joseph McMoneagle (a talented remote viewer) are of the opinion that everyone has these capabilities and can learn to do remote viewing.

Advanced Sixth Sense Experiment

If you would like to try a remote viewing session to see if you can develop this ability, I have included the steps you can take in order to give it a try. You will want to try this experiment at least 21 times to increase your chances of success.

Before you try this, as always, I recommend that you write a letter to your Higher Power to ensure you are seeking a positive experience that is within His will for you. Fear, doubt, and misunderstanding won't help you. They will only ensure failure. We all seem to have been created with these magnificent abilities; certainly our Higher Power can help us to use these abilities in the right way. Here's a sample letter you may want to write.

Dear Higher Power,

I am about to try an experiment to test the ability of the sixth sense for myself. I am human and I don't fully understand this stuff but it does seem possible we were created with this ability. If this is true, please help me to prove it to myself convincingly. I ask you to remove my fears, doubts and misunderstanding so I can have the cleanest shot at making this work. If this is ok with you, I ask you to grant me great success in this experiment. I also ask you to help me understand the best possible use of this ability. If this gift can help increase my communication with you, help me to develop it for that purpose as well. Please inspire me and protect me as I try this experiment. Thank you for your great wisdom, guidance, protection and help in all these things.

Love,
Sign Your Name

Remote Viewing Experiment

1. Have a friend select a picture or an object with simple but well defined features. This could be anything at all, just make sure it has definable shapes and texture to it as well as a few different colors if possible. After your friend

selects the item that is to be your viewing target, you will both need to agree upon a date and time when your friend will reveal this viewing target to you by actually showing it to you. This is known as the feedback time. Your friend should not give you any hints and you shouldn't ask for any. You will only find out what the item is at the agreed upon feedback time.

2. Go into a relaxed state of meditation. While you are in a relaxed state, mentally project yourself forward in time to the agreed upon feedback time when you will actually see your viewing target. In your relaxed state ask yourself what the target looks like? What does it feel like, smell like, taste like? Is it light or dark, soft or hard? What shapes do you sense? Relax and blank out your mind totally, keep it blank until you receive flashes of insight. Your first impressions and your most unusual impressions will likely be the most accurate. During the entire process never try to guess what the item is, only record the shapes and other things that you sense through your intuition.

3. Write down and draw pictures of everything you sense. Relax again and blank out your mind until you receive additional flashes of information. Write them down and draw them on paper. Repeat the process until you get no further insights.

4. At the appointed feedback time bring your notes and pictures and compare them to what your friend reveals to you as your viewing target. See how many similarities there are between what you sensed and the real object. Don't be surprised if you actually get a lot of things right!

Intelligent energy is vibrating all around us. All we need to do is slowdown and listen to our sixth sense. This can be a valuable source of otherwise unrealized information. Successful executives follow their intuition. The same goes for top salespeople, negotiators, and troubleshooters. When we learn to tune-in to our gut and interpret what it's telling us, it gives us an extra advantage in life. When we use these gifts to benefit others, they become useful tools that will also benefit us. Listed below are some other methods you can use for developing your intuitive skills.

Developing Intuition through playing games

Practicing intuitive games can be another fun way to begin strengthening your intuitive ability.

Don't worry about success or failure at this point, just have fun. Babe Ruth hit a record number of home runs but he also had a huge strikeout rate. Practice brings improvement.

Try These Exercises:

- Relax for a moment and then try sensing who the next caller will be to ring your phone.

- Relax and sense what parking spot you will get when you arrive at work or a favorite restaurant.

- When playing board games, relax and sense what number you will get on your next spin or on the next role of the dice.

- Next time you're going to a party relax and sense what topics of discussion will come up other than the normal or usual topics.

- Relax and sense how much of a raise you're getting next time raises are do. You may want to use a little mind over matter first to envision a huge raise. Just make sure you really deserve it.

- Ask someone to take a small object with well definable features and have them hide it in a box. Relax and mentally project into the box and then describe what you're sensing about the contents of the box.

When you have successes, relax to a meditative state and ask yourself "What did I do this time that helped me to get that right?" Listen for answers. Ask yourself, "How can I improve my ability of sensing and interpreting intuitive information." Don't worry about success rates, just have fun and examine any positive results in order to learn and improve. Intuition games will help strengthen your intuitive muscles.

Develop Your Intuition While You Sleep

Another way to develop intuitive ability is to use your subconscious mind to help you solve problems while you sleep. Whenever you're seeking an answer to a problem try the following. Before you fall asleep, examine all of the known elements of a specific problem or dilemma you're facing.

Write a letter or pray to your Higher Power asking for help and inspiration on how to resolve the issue. Then go to sleep. Have paper and pencil at the ready. Many times you will receive a solution the very same night. Other times you may have to repeat this exercise several times for the same problem. Answers will come. A little persistence will pay big dividends.

It has been reported that men such as Albert Einstein and Thomas Edison often received a breakthrough idea by entering a deeply relaxed state of mind and contemplating what to do.

In a state of sleep or deep relaxation they received flashes of insight that allowed them to solve a particular problem and develop solutions that have served all of mankind for many years. Developing your natural born intuitive superpowers will improve your performance and increase your ability to accomplish great things.

The next step in the SUPERMAN formula will allow you to put your new-found superhuman abilities on steroids. You will do that by improving and refining your ability to access the Highest Power in the universe for guidance, wisdom, and for additional power to achieve the best possible results in life.

Chapter 9: "Expertise of Accessing Higher Power – Experience The Benefit Of Powerful Communication With A Friend In High Places"

Improving the Process of Higher Communication

By now you've already realized some benefit from communicating with a Higher Power for good. If you followed the suggestions at the end of Chapter 3 and began to write letters to your Higher Power, you've probably already noticed some very positive results in your life.

I hope you also wrote letters to your Higher Power before the exercises of discovering your unique value and finding your passion and purpose. If you are a skeptic by nature, you may be wondering how much your little notes have really helped. One thing's for sure, it certainly didn't hurt and it most likely enhanced the benefit's you've received to this point.

At any rate those little letters were just a start. Writing your first few notes opened up the possibility of connecting with a Power that can really help you. That's all we wanted to accomplish initially. Now it's time to improve upon your starting point so you can begin seeing more and more tangible benefits in your life.

The best way to build a relationship with your Higher Power is by communicating with it every day. Communicate as often as possible throughout your day.

As with all relationships good communication will enhance a relationship, poor communication will doom it to failure. Make a commitment to yourself to spend time each day communicating with your Higher Power.

Perception Benefits Belief

Before we look at improving the way we communicate with our Higher Power there are a few things we need to understand and believe about It. We've seen in previous chapters that what we believe really has an affect for good or bad on everything we do. We've also seen that the best results for any situation will only come if we're positively focused.

This principle also applies to how we view our Higher Power. That being said, it's important to keep the following perspective as you develop your relationship with your Higher Power. The better your mindset toward your Higher Power the greater the results you'll experience. Try to develop the following mindset toward your Higher Power.

- It's on your side and wants to help you: Your Higher Power is completely on your side and wants to help you as much as you will allow. If you don't ask it for help and guidance it will leave you on your own. You have free will and your Higher Power will allow you to learn lessons from your choices. Sometimes painful ones. Seek direction and guidance from your Higher Power up front, before you make choices, and it will help if you will only listen.

- It loves you and wants you to reach your highest potential: Your Higher Power loves you as one of its greatest creations and it wants to have a working relationship with you in order to help you attain your highest potential. However you are expected to do your part of course. It helps those who help themselves. We help ourselves by seeking guidance, direction, protection and help from our Higher Power.

- You can share everything with it: You can share anything with your Higher Power without fear. It knows everything about you and understands why you are the way you are. It knows why you do the things you do. It knows that you are limited in what you can change without its help. It looks forward to helping you get over your obstacles. So share everything and ask for help!

- It doesn't hold a grudge: Your Higher Power does not hold a grudge against you. It feels sorry for you when you're hurting and when you behave in ways that harm you and others. He wants to help you and is ready to do his part if you are ready to do yours. You must be willing to take positive actions when they are revealed to you. As soon as you ask for forgiveness, you are forgiven.

- You have to do your part: You have to work at having an ongoing relationship with your Higher Power. Nobody likes being used, taken advantage of, or to be unappreciated. This principle also applies to your Higher Power. Don't just ask for help when you get yourself in a bind or when life throws you a curve. An ongoing close relationship with your Higher Power will always bring the greatest results in your life. It's a lot easier for your Higher Power to pay attention to you if you are close to it.

- You can ask for anything your heart desires: You do have to ask. You can ask for anything, there are no restrictions. Sometimes you'll get what you ask for and sometimes you won't. You just won't get things unless they're in your best interest and in the best interest of others. We don't always have the inside track on what's best for us so we need to accept that our Higher Power does. Having the right perspective toward your Higher Power will help you to grow and prosper in leaps and bounds.

Guidelines for Higher Communication

With a positive perspective towards your Higher Power your communication will automatically improve. No matter how you communicate with your Higher Power there are some general guidelines that can be very helpful for communicating more effectively. By following the guidelines listed below you will begin to notice some powerful improvement in your relationship with your Higher Power.

- Always be open and completely honest. Be yourself and try to remain as a little child. Open, honest, curious and sincere.

- Clarify your communication; be totally clear about what you want and why you want it. Communicate what you would like to happen.

- Release all negative subconscious thinking and doubt related to your request. Forgive others and yourself for all past wrongs. Accept that your Higher Power has forgiven you and no longer remembers wrongs done. Every day is a fresh start.

- Energize your request with powerful emotion and strong desire.

- Believe what you are asking for is entirely possible and that if your intent is pure it is highly probable to occur. If you don't believe it can happen it probably won't. Think of all the reasons why it can happen and focus only on them.

- Expect your request to be answered in a way that is ultimately best for you and everyone else involved.

- Let go completely of thinking about the outcome and trust that what is best for you will happen.

Honesty is the best policy in every relationship. It builds trust and closeness. We need to release any fear we have of communicating with our Higher Power. Keep in mind that an all-knowing being would know more about us than we know about ourselves. It would know our strengths, weaknesses, and our stupid human tricks.

Let's keep a constructive perspective. Our Higher Power wants to help us and is glad when we ask for help. We need to be totally trusting and without fear. The starting point is to be totally honest.

Our goal is simply to develop a strong relationship with the Highest Power there is. We really don't have a much better choice if we want to fulfill our highest potential, and if we want to live the most fulfilling life we're capable of.

We may not always be capable of reaching our objectives on our own because of our limitations. Many things will happen throughout our lives that will test our limited power, bringing us to the realization that we are totally powerless over some things. Real help is what we need when we're unable to help ourselves, and we will find real help with our Higher Power. That's truly great news.

Intense Passionate Prayer

In earlier chapters you were introduced to the method of writing letters to your Higher Power as a means of communication. Now let's take a quick look at another option.

There's something to be said for intensely throwing your heart, feelings, and emotions into any form of communication. Passionate, intense and moving, are words that describe this form of communiqué. This is the method of the greatest speakers and writers alike.

Passionate emotional communication resonates with power. It moves us to tears and motivates us to change. It charges everyone who takes it in. There is power, real power in words when they are charged with emotion and feeling.

Heartfelt prayer can be very effective. Miraculous things have happened in response to this type of intense focused energy. Sick people have been healed; impossible situations have been changed for the better and so on.

We don't always get the answer we want, but the more we go to this level the more successes we will likely have. The basic elements of this powerful communication are, focusing your thoughts on a specific request and highly charging them with emotion and intense feeling. In this mode we seem to vibrate our communication with every fiber of our body.

This type of communication is loud and clear and often receives a powerful response. It isn't necessary to work this up every time you communicate but I think you get the idea. The more you pour yourself into your prayer the more effective it will be. Your emotional state resonates through. A clear well thought out request, charged with intense emotional desire is the most powerful way to communicate with your Higher Power.

I recall the times when I was on the extreme downside of life. Especially right before my life began to change for the better. This was the kind of communication that flowed from my entire being. I cried out in despair, I was angry at God and I hated Life. I shouted and cried. I poured out my heart completely.

I asked why, and I wanted answers. I was open and honest and completely real. No halfhearted pious talk, it was completely unconventional. Respectful but without fear. I desperately needed help and I had a strong desire to know how to change.

As a result of these intense prayers and the willingness of my Higher Power to help me, here I am. Even though I wasn't worth the effort by human standards, help came through. Unlike many of my former addict buddies, today I am alive, productive and providing value to others. Before, I wasn't even of value to myself.

Today I'm blessed and happy, living a life many could scarcely imagine. Yes there is power in prayer when they're charged with honest heartfelt emotion.

There is a cleansing that takes place in this scenario, a healing and a bridging of the gap between you and your Higher Power. Next time you need to communicate with your Higher Power, try this intense form of communication and enjoy the powerful results!

Passionate Written Prayer

Emotion, feelings and focused thought can also be expressed in the written word. Writing down what's on your mind can be incredibly effective in helping to clarify your thought process.

You can be open and honest about your feelings. You can express your emotions fully. That's one of the reasons I think people develop relationships over the Internet so easily. Something about not being face-to-face makes it easier to share openly and honestly, without fear.

Too bad people don't communicate more with their spouses via email or texting. Writing a letter to the Highest Power in the universe may seem a little silly or naïve but it truly is powerful. It allows you to become like a little child. There's wonder, anticipation, hope, and of course full expression that can be involved with writing a request for help. It's actually a fun way to communicate.

The following is an actual letter I wrote to my Higher Power prior to writing this book and prior to having the idea to create my first self-improvement website.

Remember to always put your letters in your own words in order to achieve the most effective communication. Strive to apply the guidelines in this chapter, and then witness firsthand the incredible power of effective prayer.

Dear Higher Power

Thank you for all the unseen and often unappreciated help you have given me. Thanks for all of the good things you provide. I am asking you for help in the following situation as I really need your help to accomplish something I believe is worthwhile.

I want to write a book that will benefit many people. I know how much you have helped me and I know how much help others need. I'm asking for inspiration in writing the most powerful and effective self-help book possible.

If it's okay with you, please help me to receive all the ideas, motivation, ability and help I will need to see this through to completion. I ask to receive the needed connections, contacts, lucky brakes, and whatever else I will need to accomplish this great task. Please provide me with the absolute best writing style for this book and help me to complete it in the quickest time possible with my limited time.

I also ask that you provide the best methods for mass marketing this book. The main request is to ensure this book is of the greatest benefit to the most people possible. I need a lot of help as you know and I ask you to take care of as many details as possible in the background, organizing and ensuring its success. I also ask you to affect excellent timing for the completion of this writing and for its release to the public.

Please ensure the highest quality outcome and benefit to all. If this is not acceptable to you or is contrary to what is best for myself and others, please help me to see and accept that. If that is the case, please work out every detail to help me successfully pursue something even greater than this.

If this is okay with you, please help me to achieve it wonderfully, proving to the many, your great love and power. Let this be to your honor, full of truth, insight, wisdom, and real power for effecting good.

Thank you so much for your loving guidance, your patience and help. Your will be done.

Love and respect,
Mark Edward Duin

I firmly believe that this book, my other books and publications, my speaking engagements, and my online and offline businesses are the answers to this request. I had originally requested help with a book but was granted much more than I originally envisioned.

I fully believe this book has value that will help make a difference in the lives of those who read it. That's my pure desire. This book is the answer to my prayer, and that's a pretty good answer.

How many people ever write a book or a training course that helps others? How many writers actually get published? Somewhere in the neighborhood of 98% of all books never get published. If you're reading this, it means this book has been published in some fashion.

Granted, my request was not answered exactly as I had envisioned, however it has been answered in an even better fashion. Not only do I have this writing published, I have the means to provide future writings to a large audience. I am able to help a broader audience. From where I sit, this is a miracle! It's an even better outcome than I could have imagined at the time of my request. Can a power greater than you help you do what you're unable to do on your own? You can count on it.

A Clean Conscience Increases The Power of Prayer

The subconscious mind seems to play a role in our communication with our Higher Power. If we're feeling guilty, angry, doubting, or having any other negative thoughts or emotions, it seems to sabotage the effectiveness of our request. There's an appropriate religious statement that may have some validity here. "The prayers of the righteous accomplish much." And what does that mean?

If we're holding a grudge against ourselves for any reason, if we are purely being selfish without regard to others, or if we are bitter towards others, we aren't right with ourselves or our Higher Power. When we're not right with ourselves or our Higher Power we don't feel, deep down, that we deserve what we are asking for. If we don't feel we deserve what we're asking for, we probably won't receive it.

So, what can we do to cleanse our thoughts and feelings from the negative crud that's buried inside us? Actually it's much easier than you would imagine. In the next Chapter on Release we'll cover this in greater detail, for now simply write out all the things that are bugging you right now.

This simple little exercise has a very cleansing and healing affect. Try this, set a timer for five minutes. Write at the top of a piece of paper the question, "What's bugging me now?" Start the timer and write as fast as you can for five minutes, everything that bugs you. Don't stop to think about it, just write. As you write, feel the release of all the negative thoughts feelings and emotions, the doubts and fears. Just write and write until you get it all out of you. Now you're ready to more effectively communicate with your Higher Power.

Communication Outline

Use the steps listed below to improve the way you communicate with your Higher Power. This outline will help you to use what you've learned in this chapter.

Step 1. Get Ready. Before you start any communication, verbal, mental or written, with your Higher Power, take a minute to remember to be as a little child, open, honest and free from fear.

Step 2. Address your Higher Power with respect, be thankful for the opportunity to have a relationship with the Highest Power there is.

Step 3. Clarify; be totally clear about what you want and why you want it. Think about what you want to talk about before you start so that you're organized and clear as you communicate with your Higher Power.

Step 4. Energize your request with focused thought, powerful emotion and a strong feeling of desire.

Step 5. Release all negative subconscious thinking and doubt related to your request. Forgive and forget about your past failings and the failings of others.

Step 6. Believe that what you are asking for is entirely possible and that if your intention is pure it is highly probable to occur.

Step 7. Expect your request to be answered in a way that is ultimately best for you and everyone else involved. Let go completely of thinking about the outcome. Trust that what is best for all will happen.

Reliance on a Higher Power is the most powerful tool known to man. It's a free gift for your benefit. Develop a relationship with your Higher Power and you'll quickly realize just what a tremendous blessing it is. Use this outline in all your communications with your Higher Power and you'll experience a wonderful new life of powerful positive change!

Combining Superpowers

Imagine the force of combining the abilities of mind over matter and intuition with the power and direction of a Higher Power for good. Throw in your unique talents, experiences, skills, your driving passion and purpose.

Combine these all together and you're ready to kick some mediocre living in the butt. Wow talk about progress, you're only three-quarters of the way through the book and the superhero is taking shape. You can't stop now though you're only part way done.

Get ready to gain new freedom and to make greater advances than ever before, by discovering and releasing the internal enemies that have held you back from becoming all you can be.

<u>R</u> - Release

Chapter 10: "Release Your Internal Enemies – Get Rid Of The Negative Subconscious Thinking That Secretly Prevents Your Success!"

Hidden Enemies

Negative experiences throughout our lives accumulate and join forces to become our internal enemies. The longer we've been around the more enemy baggage we're likely to carry. These enemies are just puffed up bags of hot air, but we seem to give them the power to wreck our lives.

And what are these self-saboteurs? Guilt, fear, regret, anger, bitterness, envy, grief, loneliness, arrogance, and doubt, to name a few. Ouch, now there's a nasty group of words. These internal enemies can be very evasive and covert.

We usually don't realize they're hiding within us. Oh but they are there. All too often they're carrying out their sneaky little attacks, telling us we're not good enough, that we're going to fail or that we don't deserve better. Causing extensive damage a little bit at a time.

Searching out these damaging enemies needs to be a top priority. We've got to dig them out of their hiding places so we can see them for what they are and so we can put them in their proper place.

If we don't, they'll continue their destructive attacks on us, robbing us of our great potential and causing us unnecessary difficulties.

We need to destroy these enemies so they don't cause us anymore pain. With these enemies out of the way we're no longer held captive by false thinking, we have a full release. Complete freedom is what we feel.

You can't imagine the complete feeling of freedom and elation you'll experience once they're gone. Wide-open fields of opportunity will lay before you. The saboteurs that once prevented you from greater success will no longer exist. You'll be free to hit the ground running. You can now go farther in life, faster than ever before.

How can you discover these enemies and get rid of them? It all starts by closely examining your life. Don't cut corners on this process, half-hearted effort will provide half-hearted results. The more thorough you are the greater your rewards will be.

Remember, there's nothing more precious than your life. It's important to do the things that will allow you to become your best. This step is of major importance for getting rid of the self-limiting thoughts and behaviors that have been sabotaging your life.

Preparation and Initial Instructions

In just a few minutes I'll be listing the major internal enemies that negatively impact most people. Each one will be followed by some simple instructions that will help you discover and root out any troublemakers you may have.

As you go through the instructions, take a look back over your life in ten-year increments, for example from ages 1-10, 10 to 20, then ages 20 to 30 and so on until you reach your current age.

For each question asked, apply that question for each ten-year period. Look for anything you can remember for those time periods that relate to fear, guilt, anger and so on. Write down everything you can remember relating to each question as far back as you can remember. If something comes to mind it's probably something that bothers you. Write down everything that comes to mind and remember, your list is just between you and your Higher Power.

This exercise is designed to help you break through old barriers so you can move to a higher level of living. This is real self-discovery and it's very personal. In some cases you will be examining your behavior and asking the questions, "why did I do that?", "what was I trying to gain?" It could be you were just needing attention or maybe you were just plain curious. Often when we internalize things we tend to blow them out of proportion. Don't think about it too much just list everything that comes to mind.

After you complete this exercise, examine your lists and see if you notice any trends. Trends can help you identify problems. Note any recurring problems so you can begin to look for solutions. Keep in mind that no matter what has happened or what you've done, no matter how bad it seems, realize that many other people have experienced the same things or worse. There are billions of people in the world and you are just another human being sharing the common experience of living.

You're not bad or evil but you may have made some poor choices just like I have, as well as everyone else. You can't change what's happened, it's over and done. However you can change how your past will affect your future.

The objective of this exercise is to rid yourself of any negative self-limiting thinking and to turn your past negative experiences into something positive.

Seek Higher Help & Guidance

Before you begin, write a letter to your Higher Power asking for help and guidance in releasing your hidden enemies. Ask to learn what you can that will benefit your future. Ask for and accept complete forgiveness for all the wrongs you've done and ask for help to completely forgive yourself. Forgive anyone who has harmed you and ask your Higher Power to help them and bless them.

Search Out and Destroy the Enemy

Let's get to the task at hand. Your time is your life, and your life is too valuable to waist on fear, regret, anger, loneliness or any other thief that steals away from real living. This is a simple exercise that will pay huge dividends for the rest of your life.

Read the following paragraphs that describe common things that can get you into trouble. Simply follow the instructions at the end of each description and start enjoying the freedom that results.

Shame, Guilt, and Regret

Shame, guilt, and regret are several internal tools that can turn into enemies. Whenever we violate our conscience or whenever we wrong someone else, deep down we feel it.

Sometimes we may think we can suppress shame and guilt without any consequence but our subconscious mind always knows what we've done. Shame and guilt are an internal way of letting us know we've harmed our character or our fellow man.

Our conscience is guiding us and trying to protect us, it's trying to steer us away from behavior that harms us and others. Committing an act that we know is wrong will come back to haunt us. Poor behavior complicates our lives because eventually our actions catch up with us.

Unfortunately each of us has made our share of mistakes. Throughout our lives we do a number of things that we don't feel good about. Our subconscious always knows what we've done and we end up holding these things against ourselves. Until we find a way to root out our shame, guilt, and regret, we'll often sabotage ourselves without even realizing it.

Of course the best way to avoid these enemies is to never do anything wrong in the first place. We should constantly strive to do what we know to be right at all times. However the reality is that we're still human and bound to make mistakes. It is for our times of failing that we need to find a way to gain freedom from these internal enemies.

Ask yourself the following questions and write down the answers. Take any of the suggested steps listed on the next pages to rid yourself of unproductive shame guilt and regret.

Write down everything you have ever done that you are ashamed of and ask yourself the following questions in relation to each thing you list:

- Why do I think I did these things, what was I trying to gain?

- What happened as a result of my actions, what did I really get?
- What valuable lesson can I gain from these experiences?
- What could I do better in the future? What will I gain from taking a better approach?

Grief

Grief is an important mechanism that helps us deal with the shocking things in life. Grief is the emotion that helps us deal with the loss of something or someone we love or are attached to. It shows us our absolute powerlessness in certain situations and causes us to search beyond ourselves for answers. Grief is powerful and it affects us deeply. It shows us how much we care and that we are connected to things outside of us.

After we've been through a grieving process we experience a deeper appreciation for our own life and for the lives of others. There is definitely a time to grieve. There is also a time to stop grieving so we can continue to live.

We need to deal thoroughly with grief, working all the way through it so we can move on. Sometimes we suppress our grief, we try to cut corners because we don't want to feel the pain. Unfortunately this harms us and eventually others. It stunts our emotional growth. Suppressed grief can lead to prolonged sadness, anger, and bitterness.

To be sure these feelings are all part of the grieving process, but we need to work through these emotions during the grieving process or else we'll end up dealing with them over a longer period of time. When we continually have these emotions to deal with we can't enjoy life. It's important to prevent grief from becoming an enemy.

Ask yourself the following questions and write down the answers on a separate piece of paper. Take any other suggested steps listed on the next page to help you get to the other side of the grieving process.

As mentioned before grief is a powerful and complex emotion. We recommend that you seek out a grief counselor to help you work through all the stages of grief.

- What am I grieving over?
- Why am I still grieving?
- Is it still time to grieve?
- Am I ready to move on?
- What are some better ways for me to deal with this?

Arrogance and Self-Serving

Self-reliance is a skill we must learn in order to do our part. It starts when we are very young. We learn to get dressed by ourselves, to tie our shoes, then we progress to holding a job and paying the bills. We need to pull our own weight so we're not a burden on others.

Being reliable and responsible gives us a healthy self-worth. We know we're contributing and that we're providing value and earning what we receive. We feel good about ourselves.

Unfortunately there may be times when we take self-reliance to the extreme. We may begin to think we're a little more important than we are. As much as we would like to think otherwise, we actually receive a lot of help from others. In fact, everything we have or use is provided by the efforts of others. That is of course unless we grow our own food, make our own material and clothing, design and build our own homes and cars, and create and manufacture everything else we use on a daily basis.

We sometimes forget our limits and we want to be put on a pedestal. We may think the world owes us somehow and that without our incredible greatness the world would be at a loss. Pride comes before a fall. False pride alienates us from others. It causes us to miss out on the opportunities and joys that other people add to our lives.

We can get ourselves in quite a bit of trouble if we become arrogant and self-centered. This enemy is very misleading. It paints a pretty picture then turns ugly real fast.

Ask yourself the following questions and write down the answers. Take any other suggested steps to help you get rid of arrogance and self-serving.

- How have I been arrogant and self-serving?
- What was I trying to gain by this behavior, what did I feel I was lacking?
- What did I actually get as a result of my behavior?
- What can I learn of value from these experiences?
- What are some better ways for me to deal with this?

Loneliness and Self Pity

Loneliness is another feeling that can really take away from the enjoyment of life. If loneliness serves any purpose at all, it's to tell us that we're disconnected from the world around us, and that we need to find a way to get reconnected. It urges us to get involved with acts of service, especially service that will help those who are less fortunate. It urges us to reach out and connect to others through organizations, work, family and social situations.

When we allow loneliness to fester in us instead of following its urging, we begin to close ourselves off from the world. When we do this we can feel all alone in a room full of people. We become totally immersed in ourselves and we sever all connections to the outside world. We become full of self-pity.

Our priorities get messed up and we begin to think we're all there is. We get sad, mad and depressed because the world doesn't take note of us. We forget that the needs of others are equal to our own. We forget that happiness comes from loving and serving others more so than from being loved or served by others.

Loneliness is an enemy that sidetracks our focus and robs us of the joy we would receive by going outside of ourselves. It robs others of the value we could bring to them through the love and service we could provide.

Ask yourself the following questions and write down the answers. Take any other suggested steps to help you get rid of loneliness.

- How have I let loneliness and self-pity take control of me?
- What was it that I really wanted, what was I trying to get?
- What did I actually get from my lonely thought process and self-

isolation?
- What can I learn of value from these experiences?
- What are some better ways for me to deal with this?

Anger, Bitterness, and Resentment

Anger is a powerful tool of expression. We use it to let others know we've been wronged, that an injustice has taken place. We use anger to attempt to correct others by showing them the gravity of their offense.

Anger is sometimes justified but not always. Anger is very volatile and can easily be misdirected. There is a time to be angry and a time to forgive and forget. With no small effort, we can bring ourselves to forgive almost anything.

I know that's a difficult statement as there are so many horrendous things people can do, but we really have to bring ourselves to forgive if we want to be free. Not for the benefit of the offender but for our own benefit and wellbeing.

It's for our own peace of mind so the offender doesn't win. If we stay angry, bitter and resentful, our lives are ruined as long as we're in that state. The person or situation that caused our anger may not be affected at all, they continue on, no sweat off their back. Meanwhile our blood boils and we plot revenge or at least think nasty thoughts. We're tied up in knots whenever the issue comes to mind. Our anger hurts us.

How can we live a joyful, peaceful, productive life with this enemy destroying us from within? We need to root this enemy all the way out so we can live our life in peace instead of turmoil. One good thing to keep in mind is that what goes around comes around; we don't have to take ownership of justice. Those who wrong us will meet their own fate. They will suffer the consequences of their own actions. We just can't let their wrong ways ruin our quality of life by staying mad.

Ask yourself the following questions and write down the answers. Take any other suggested steps to help you get rid of anger, bitterness, and resentment.

- What am I angry, bitter, or resentful about?
- How have I acted out anger, bitterness and resentment?
- What was I trying to gain from my actions, what was I trying to get?
- What did I actually get from acting out my anger, bitterness, or resentment?
- What can I learn of value from these experiences?
- What are some better ways for me to deal with this?

Doubt

Doubt is supposed to help protect us from doing unrealistic or dangerous things. It's okay to doubt our ability to stop a moving train by standing in front of it. Or to doubt you could fly without some external apparatus like a plane.

Doubt should help prevent us from rushing into anything without understanding all the facts. Once we have all the facts, doubt can help temper our approach. Of course when we look at the facts we need to be sure not to focus on just the negative, but the positive facts as well.

For example, before airplanes were invented there were plenty of so-called facts that said man should not fly. Many a person said, "If man were meant to fly he'd been born with wings". There was also evidence to suggest that it was possible for man to fly. After all birds could fly and flying squirrels could at least float through the air. Why couldn't a craft be built with wings and an engine that could fly a human being? When we only look at the negative biased side of things we allow doubt to kill our drive and our dreams. We prevent ourselves from pursuing our hearts desire. Who knows how many dreams doubt has killed.

We need to examine where we've allowed doubt to steal away from our fulfillment. We need to find out what's been holding us back? We need to focus on why things can be accomplished instead of why they can't. This is the mind we need to strive for.

Ask yourself the following questions and write down the answers. Take any other suggested steps to help you get over doubt.

- How have I let doubt prevent me from pursuing something great?
- What was I trying to accomplish by doubting?
- What was the end result of my doubt?
- What are some better ways for me to deal with this?

Fear and Worry

Fear is an inborn gift that can be of great benefit to us. If we're trying to cross a street and about halfway across we hear a vehicle roaring towards us, we can respond to our fear by jumping out of the way. If we're driving along a mountain road with a deep cliff just over the edge, our fear should help us drive carefully around those corners. Healthy fears protect us.

It's the unhealthy fears that cause us all the problems. I once heard a speaker say that over 90 percent of the things people fear or worry about never happen. Of the 10 percent of legitimate fears people have, we can actually do something about 6 percent of those. Of the remaining 4 percent, we can't do anything about them anyway, so why waste time worrying about them.

Let's take a look at a common fear. Let's say the fear of flying for example. For this example let's use someone who has to fly 60 days per year. Every time this person has to fly they are filled with anxiety for the entire day.

They work themselves up over their fear of flying. The facts show that the odds are better than a million to one this person will never get into a plain wreck. This fear falls well into the 90 percent of fears that will never happen. In this example our flight fearing friend will have literally wasted two months of their life on unproductive anxiety filled days for no reason.

Almost all of us carry around a little bag of fears on a frequent basis. Worries are subtle enemies that steal away from our ability to be happy and productive. Unhealthy fear and worry takes the joy out of living. We need to strive to keep ourselves free of worry and fear in order to enjoy our limited time for living.

Ask yourself the following questions and write down the answers. Take any other suggested steps that are listed to rid you of unproductive fear and worry.

- What have I been afraid of and what have I wasted time worrying about?
- Which of my fears or worries fall into the 90% that will most likely never happen?

- Of my fears and worries, what do I have control over?
- What is the absolute worst thing that could happen if my fears really happen?
- What productive steps can I take to address the things I do have control over?

Envy

Envy is the final enemy we want to confront in this chapter. It's healthy to want to be more, to accomplish more, and to attain the best we're capable of. Not being totally satisfied with where we are helps drive us to do greater things. But when we're ungrateful for what we do have and we become excessively obsessed with wanting more than we have, that's when we've crossed over to the dark side. Envy is the great broker of dissatisfaction and unhappiness. The grass is always greener on the other side. When we are stuck in envy, whatever we attain it's never good enough, we take for granted what we do have and think that having more will fix us.

Sometimes we even want things we can't or shouldn't have. Things that aren't in our best interest to have. Unfortunately the wrong things can never give us what we really want, satisfaction. We fail to realize that satisfaction comes from giving of ourselves. Envy is an enemy that keeps us off-track. It keeps us chasing after things that can never give us what we want.

When we take time to focus on our many blessings we begin to see that we have an abundance of things. The average person in the whole world (including Third World countries) makes something less than $1200 per year. They don't have the luxuries we do. They often don't even have the basic needs of food, water and shelter. Below the average person is the below average person who has even less. That thought alone should make us shutter, drop to our knees, and cry out in gratitude for the wonderful things we do have.

If more stuff hasn't satisfied us yet, getting even more stuff won't do the trick. Envy is a deceptive life-wasting enemy. We need to realize how envy has really kept us from enjoying what we do have. It causes us to fill our lives with emptiness.

Ask yourself the following questions and write down the answers. Take any other suggested steps to help you get over envy.

- How have I let envy take control of me?
- What was it that I really wanted, what was I trying to get?
- What was the actual result of my envy?
- What can I learn of value from these experiences?
- What can I do in the future to make things better?
- Who have I offended or hurt as a result of my envy?
- What is in my power to do, to make amends for any harm I have caused?
- What are some better ways for me to deal with this?

This release exercise should open your eyes to the types of enemies that lurk about, stealing your happiness at every opportunity. From now on, as soon as you catch yourself not feeling great, look through this list of enemies and identify and eliminate them right away. Life's too short to stay out of sorts.

As a final catch all and as sort of a spot check inventory you can use almost anytime, ask yourself the following questions before you go to sleep every night and at odd moments throughout your day.

What's bugging me now?
Why does it bother me, what's the real issue for me?
What positive things can I do about it?
What do I need to let go of?
What do I need to accept?
Who do I need to forgive?
Have I harmed anyone?
How can I make restitution?

Release the Enemies and Gain Your Freedom

Once you've completed the exercise in this chapter, read over and examine everything you've written, learn what you can, then destroy everything you've written in regards to your internal enemies. You shred them into a million pieces, bury them, or whatever else you want to do to release them forever. For those who believe in confession, this would be a good list to take for that purpose before you destroy the list.

Selfishness and self-centeredness are at the root of almost all human troubles. Freedom from these internal enemies will give you more abundant satisfying living.

You can't become a superhero by being selfish or self-serving. Real superheroes are selfless; they only focus on helping and serving others. Re-do the exercise in this chapter at least twice per year and preferably quarterly in order to do a major house cleaning of your internal enemies.

When you do, you'll feel clean, fresh, renewed. Now quickly review your strengths list, your passion and purpose statement and make a commitment to yourself to live a positive new life from now on. Now you can go forward enjoying the powerful freedom from burden and self-restriction you once suffered from. There is no stopping you now, you're flying high. Turn to the next chapter and get ready to Make A Difference in this world!

<u>M</u> - Make a Difference

Chapter 11: "Make A Difference In Your World – Gain A Place In History As A Positive Difference Maker!"

Get Ready to Make a Difference

You are now armed with access to some incredible superpowers, you've gained insight into your great value, you've discovered passion and purpose for your life and you've destroyed the internal enemies that used to hold you back. You're now ready to focus on how you can make a difference.

You have everything you need to start making an incredible difference in the world as you rack up fantastic accomplishments. From now on, the more you align your will with the will of the Highest Power for good the more of a difference you'll find yourself making.

Change, significant change, starts with one person. When the human mind locks onto a worthy cause, it begins to creatively think of ways to make it happen. The individual who is charged with passion and purpose and who is armed with a strategy to bring it into reality is bound to become a superhero.

Our world sure could use a few good superheroes. You're now up to the challenge. You know almost anything is possible and that the truly worthy goal will get a lot of help from the greatest superpower there is.

Individuals Make The Difference

All humanly created things started in someone's mind. The idea for cars, airplanes, air conditioning, computers, telephones, washers and dryers, hair dryers, staple guns, television, stereos, tractors, transport trucks, headphones, skyscrapers, artificial limbs, heart transplants, the dictionary, windshield wipers, everything created by humans started in the mind of a an individual.

Idea originators combine their ideas with the know-how of other individuals and working together they make a huge difference in the world providing tremendous value to their fellow human beings. Without individuals to come up with original ideas, progress comes to a halt. Without individuals to make an idea into reality, progress comes to a halt. Ordinary individuals just like you and I make an incredible difference by using their incredible abilities

Many people become great contributors by simply improving things that already exist. For example, Thomas Edison's light bulb was not really the first light bulb. Mr. Edison improved upon the original idea by finding a way to make it practical and usable by the general population. He made the idea workable. Isaac Merritt Singer is another example. Mr. Singer improved upon an existing sewing machine and was successful in making his version the commercial sewing machine. His contributions allowed for the growth of the readymade clothing industry. We all still benefit from both of these men's contributions.

People With Passion Overcome Obstacles

George Washington Carver was born into a poor black slave family in the early 1860's. As a small child he contracted whooping cough and was left in a weakened state. He was unable to do the hard labor of the field workers. Instead he did the inside chores of sewing, cooking and also gardening.

George taught himself to read and at about age 12 he went to a one-room schoolhouse that had one teacher for about 75 children. Talk about poor Teacher to student ratio. During recess he stayed inside and studied because he had a passion for knowledge. He was accepted to College University and was later rejected when they discovered his race. He later found his way to what is now known as Iowa State University where he earned his bachelor's and master's degrees.

Our poor, black, unhealthy Mr. Carver developed methods for crop rotation that revolutionized the agricultural industry. He didn't let his obstacles hold him back. He worked his own way through college doing any job he could find to pay his way. Mr. Carver developed over 300 uses for peanuts including cooking oil, soap and printers ink. He developed another 100 products from sweet potatoes and 75 products from pecans. One man with a very humble beginning and enormous obstacles found his passion in life and became a valuable superhero in the agricultural industry.

Florence Nightingale was born in Florence Italy on May 12th in 1820. She was born to a wealthy English family. Miss Nightingale's parents had planned for her to become a socialite but she found a passion that changed her direction.

Florence wanted to do something worthwhile with her life and by the age of 16 she was certain that God was guiding her to serve others. She began visiting hospitals in London and had discovered a passion for caring for the sick. Her parents did not approve and felt this behavior was unworthy of a person of her status.

Her father finally allowed her to attend a nursing school in Kaiserwerthrth Germany in 1853. In 1854 the Crimean War began. Britain, France, and Turkey had declared war on Russia.

During this war, British medical facilities were highly criticized for their handling of the wounded. Florence was asked to oversee the start of nurses in military hospitals. She led a team of 38 nurses into a British military hospital.

At first Doctors rejected the idea of female nurses, but after an enormous influx of wounded their minds were changed. The introduction of female nurses into military hospitals was an enormous success.

Florence went on to establish the Nightingale Training School for Nurses. She wrote and published over 200 books, reports and pamphlets on nursing and improving health. Her most famous work was "Notes on Nursing" that was translated into 11 foreign languages and is still in print today. She became known as the founder of modern-day nursing. Miss Nightingale found her passion for serving others and thankfully didn't let her high society status prevent her from making a lasting difference in the world.

Thomas Alva Edison was born in 1847, the last of seven children. His mother was a former schoolteacher, his father a jack of all trades. Thomas became one of the world's greatest inventors despite the fact he only had three months of formal education. During those three months his teacher thought he was a confused, mixed up kid (ADD?) incapable of learning. Mr. Edison especially didn't like Math.

In addition to his lack of formal education, Thomas was handicapped. He had experienced many childhood ear problems and was involved in an accident at the age of 15 that caused him to lose much of his hearing. Because of his deafness he liked to read. He spent a lot of time at the library and studied a variety of subjects such as mechanics, electricity, chemicals, and manufacturing.

At about the age of 9 his mother gave him a science book that included experiments. By the age of 10 he had built his first science lab in the basement. He focused his ideas and inventions on things that everyone could use. His passion was to take ideas and put them to practical use. He patented over 1,000 inventions in his lifetime. Many of his greatest inventions are still in use today in one form or another.

He paved the way for modern-day lights, recording devices, records and CDs, man-made rubber, and stock tickers. He founded the first electric power station for lights, the Edison Electric Light Company. Now known as General Electric.

Thomas Edison took a lot of risks and failed often but failing didn't seem to bother him. He always tried to learn something of value from each mistake and headed toward the next success. Real superheroes aren't problem free, they just learn to leap tall buildings and stay on course. Because of this, a poor, uneducated, deaf kid, became one of the greatest inventors of all-time. His contributions have made a huge difference in the lives of billions of people including yours and mine.

Our final example is that of Mary Anderson. Mary invented a window-cleaning device in 1903. This new innovation allowed for car drivers to clean snow, sleet and rain off of their windshield while still sitting in their automobile. Windshield wipers are of tremendous value to millions if not billions of drivers even today. What a difference a single person can make, despite gender, age, economic background, race, handicap, or any other so-called obstacles.

All of these examples involve what were just once ordinary people. Some of the greatest contributors to our world have had the greatest obstacles to overcome. The good news is that we don't have to focus on changing the world to make a difference. We just need to focus on putting our own passion, interests and strengths to good use, serving or creating value for others.

Characteristics of Difference Makers

Let's take a look at some of the characteristics of real difference makers. What separates them from the ordinary masses?

- They believe they can, their focus is on possibilities not on limitations.
- They look at what they do have rather than what they don't have.
- They discover something to be passionate about.
- They create value for others out of their passion.
- They pursue their passion every day and every opportunity they can.
- They persist until they succeed.
- They don't fear failure but rather use failure to learn lessons that will help them succeed on the next run.
- They work with and through other people to create value.
- They solve problems.
- They change lives and the world around them because of their passion.

Real life superheroes are much better than any imaginary superhero, because they are real. So many difference makers have existed throughout time we couldn't fit them all into a million volumes of books.

Human superheroes are everywhere and they are simply made up of people like us. With what you've been learning in this book you too are ready to make a difference.

Make a Difference Every Day

For starters you can create immediate value every day simply by improving your focus. Strive to greet each day with a grateful attitude. Appreciate each new day, being thankful for whatever type of day it is. Change your focus to look at what you do have, not at what you lack. Look for the good in a rainy day, the beauty in a snowy day, the awesome power of a stormy day.

Before you begin your work think of all the people who don't have a job. When you feel unhappy about growing older, think of those who have worse health than you do. Be grateful for what you do have, find the good in others and in every situation. An attitude of gratitude will make a difference in you and that in turn will make a difference to others.

Once you start to change your focus to more positive things each day, then you can begin to improve the way you interact with the people around you. From now on you can follow these steps whenever you interact with others.

- Greet every person with a sincere and loving smile, most of them will smile back.
- Treat every person as if they are the most important person you've seen.
- Get out of yourself and take a genuine interest in others. Listen to what people say and take an interest in the things that interest them.
- Encourage others to talk about their interests and admire the

twinkle in their eyes as they talk.
- Always focus on the positive qualities of others and strive to see them in that light. Point out what you like about people and encourage them by letting them know.
- Never focus on the negative qualities of others lest someone begin to focus on yours.

The way we greet our day, situations, and others, has an enormous impact. It's a very positive and simple way to impact the world in an immediate way. The world needs much more of this kind of behavior. Just a few simple steps can make you a superhero in the eyes of others on a daily basis.

Make a Difference by Using Your Strengths

Think back to chapter 5 where you began to discover your unique value. Review your strengths every day. Have them fresh at the forefront of your mind every morning. As you progress through your day look for opportunities to use your abilities to make a difference.

Cheer somebody up, provide a shoulder to cry on, help someone who can't help themselves. Keep your eyes open for the signal to jump into superhero mode. When your mind is focused on the value you can provide it gets busy looking for places to apply it. Make a difference every day with your unique gifts.

Make a Difference by Your Weakness

Relating to others who share your same weaknesses is another way to make a difference. Did you ever think your weaknesses could be used to make a difference?

Share your experience, hope and strengths with anyone you can help. People with problems and challenges need support. They need someone they can relate to. Someone who really knows what it's all about. Someone who understands what they're going through. A person who has experienced a similar weakness and has overcome it is often the only one that can truly help.

Make a Difference by Your Life Experience

Wisdom gained through all of your valuable life lessons can also be a powerful tool. The food for thought you provide to others is like planting seeds. Others may not always take your advice at first, but what you speak goes into their mind. Their subconscious picks it up.

You're helpful insights may be combined with the insights of others, and when the time is right the light bulb will come on. Planting seeds of wisdom is often a thankless and unnoticed service, but it does contribute to getting the job done.

Failures are another experience you have. Sharing the experience of your failures can help others to see that successful people also fail. The difference is that successful people work through their failures and go on to achieve great success. They learn from their mistakes and gain value from them. The more you try, the harder you try, the more successes you will have, regardless of the number of failures you encounter on the way. Encourage others by sharing your failures.

Your victories are an obvious difference maker. Sharing the experience of your victories will inspire others to do things they may have never thought possible. Your victories help others to see that they too can achieve great things. Victories are fun to share with others and almost everyone loves to hear the story of a winner.

The Rewards of Creating & Providing Value

From now on use your superpowers, your unique talents and abilities, your passion and purpose, your expertise and experience to make a difference. Give others some much needed hope inspiration and support. As you do, you create tremendous value.

Helping just 2 people per day can have an incredible impact. Open a door for someone, cause someone to smile, let someone else go first, anything that will benefit others in some way. If you help 2 people every day for a year, that would be 730 people per year. If those same 730 people are inspired by your example and in turn help 2 more people every day, well, that would be a whole lot of people. Simple things make a huge difference.

The world we live in has far too many people that don't try to make a positive difference. Unfortunately, far too many don't even care. That's the norm for now. Once you break out of the unhappy pack you can start to help the unhappy pack. Followers rarely make a huge difference.

Difference makers are leaders, true superhero's that end up blessing and benefiting others by their actions. Living closer to your superhuman potential will pay big dividends by helping to change the world for the better one day at a time. You can make a huge difference in this world and I have no doubt that you will!

<u>A</u> – Activating Action

Chapter 12: "Activate Your Action Plan – Learn To Make Sure You Achieve What You Want!"

"The victory of success is half won when one gains the habit of setting goals and achieving them. Even the most tedious chore will become endurable as you parade through each day convinced that every task, no matter how menial or boring, brings you closer to achieving your dreams." - Og Mandino 1923-1996, Author

Increase Your Success by More Than 90%!

I'm not sure this can be proven but from my own experience I believe that most super-successful people are those who have written goals. In fact the people I know who follow a goal process accomplish easily 10 times more than the majority of people who don't have goals at all. Don't let the simplicity of goals fool you. When you write down your goals, it helps your mind tune-in to achieving them.

Here is a great process for setting and achieving your goals...

Step *One: Pick The Right Goal*

The first step in the goal setting process is to pick the "Right Goal" for You! A great way to do this is to write down 21 things you want to accomplish or attain in your lifetime.

Next, cross off the three least important items. Review your list again and cross off three more items. Keep up this process until you end up with the top three things you want to accomplish or attain.

Step Two: Rank Your Goals For Attainability

The second step is to discover which goal you want badly enough to actually acquire. For this, all you need to do is rank each goal. For each of your top three goals, ask yourself the following questions.

- On a scale from 1 to 10, 1 being least and 10 being most, how important is this to me right now? Write your score next to each item.
- On a scale from 1 to 10, 1 being least and 10 being most, how much time and effort am I willing to put into attaining this right now? Write your score next to each item.
- On a scale from 1 to 10, 1 being least and 10 being most, how badly do I really want or need this right now? Write your score next to each item.

Total your score for each goal. You have a potential of 30 points for each one. Your highest scoring goal should be the best candidate for success right now. The time is right. You've picked a goal that you really want or need, it's important to you, and you are willing to put time and effort into attaining it. Go ahead and pick one of your top ranking goals and move on to the third step.

Step Three: Write It Down And Think It Through

Written Goals are the foundation of Great Accomplishment. You can use this written part of the Goal Power Strategy to accomplish almost anything.

Whether you want to improve your education, land a better job, buy a new car, obtain a specific amount of money, improve your relationships, or anything else, you can Increase your success rate by asking yourself the following questions and writing down your answers:

- I want or need the following?
- Why do I want / need this?
- What do I need in order to reach this goal?
- Why do I falsely believe this is unattainable?
- Why do I know it is actually possible to reach this or a similar objective?
- How can I use my strengths to help achieve this goal?
- How can I benefit others as a result of this goal?
- What people, organizations, books, training or any other resources are available to help me achieve this goal?
- What specific tasks need to be accomplished in order to reach this objective?
- What do I see as the greatest obstacles to achieving this goal?
- What can I do to overcome these obstacles?
- How can I keep this goal in the front of my mind every day?

Step Four: Convince Your Mind To Achieve It

This step is an absolute must do. Read your written goals 3 times per day to keep your mind focused on making them happen.

It is "Very Important" to read them just before you go to sleep and as soon as you wake up. Reading them out loud is preferred if at all possible.

These two times are when your mind is very open to the programming of suggestions. Strive to read your goals a third time somewhere in the middle of your day. Just so you don't let them get crowded out by distractions.

Develop a clear picture in your mind of what it will be like once your goal is accomplished. In your mind, vividly experience yourself as already having the thing you desire. Make this mental imagery as real as possible by using all of your senses. See it, feel it, touch it, hear it, taste it, all in your mind. Play this mental video every night before you go to sleep and every morning when you wake up. Once your subconscious mind believes "without doubt" that you will achieve your goal, you will be in the optimum mode to make it happen!

Every night before you drift off to sleep ask yourself the following question: "What can I do now to make this goal a reality?"

Step Five: Pass The Test

As an added bonus of becoming a top achiever, you will be tested. Almost like magic, as soon as you make up your mind to attain something good, obstacles appear. It's Life's little way of testing you. This test is designed to help you prove to yourself that you are committed to what you've decided upon.

Just remember for every obstacle you encounter there is a way to victory over it. Obstacles always seem a lot worse than they really are, so just stay the course and keep your goal in the front of your mind. As you do, you will find sweet victory and attain the object of your desire.

As you face obstacles, every night before you drift off to sleep ask yourself the following question: "How can I overcome this obstacle in the quickest and easiest way?"

Step Six: Act On Your Ideas

With your mind focused on accomplishing your goal, you will begin to have inspirational ideas that are in line with what you want to achieve. Whenever you get inspired with an idea that's in line with your goal, take action! Sometimes you'll get the perfect idea at the perfect time. Other times your idea will be in the right direction but you'll have to make adjustments along the way to your goal. Just keep your goal in front of your mind, follow these steps, and act when inspired, and you will accomplish far more than most than ever before.

Sample Goal Achievement Strategy

Outlined below is a goal achievement strategy that will help give you some ideas for your own strategy. I'll use an example of a goal of wanting one million dollars to help illustrate. After you review this example, use the steps listed above to map out your own goal achievement strategy for your top ranking goals.

I want or need the following?
I want $1,000,000.

Why do I want / need this?
To be financially secure so I don't have to worry about supporting my family. So I can concentrate my time and energy on something more worthwhile. So I have resources to help others.

Where am I today in relation to this goal?
Today I have a net worth of $100,000.

What do I need in order to reach this goal?
$900,000.

Why do I falsely believe this is unattainable?
That's a lot of money. I'm 42 years old and have a family to support. How could anybody get from where I am to there? The economy is down. I have no idea what I could possibly do in order to reach this goal. I have little formal education. I'm a former street kid. I have no connections.

Why do I know it is actually possible to reach this or a similar objective?
Well, there are a lot of self-made millionaires. There are even self-made billionaires. Bill Gates made multiple billions in less than 20 years. I have another 30 years to get there. There are multiple billions of dollars wasted each year by government and big business. One million dollars is nothing compared to all the money in the world. It's actually very small.

There are Trillions of dollars and more sitting unused in banks and financial institutions all around the world. Money that could be used to help others. My intentions are noble and I can ask my Higher Power for anything. He may not grant it, but I can ask. I can hope. I know that anything is possible with my Higher Power. I guess I will make a request and see what happens. I do believe that this is not as outrageous as I had first thought.

What request can I write my Higher Power?

Dear Higher Power,

As you know I think I want one million dollars in order to have increased financial security for my family and so that I can pursue more worthwhile goals of service.

I also would be able to offer greater financial support to those in need. Of all the wasted money in the world I feel that a million dollars is not too much to ask for, and that a lot of good could be accomplished with it in the right hands. If this would be in line with your will for me, I ask that you grant this request and I ask for your help to put this to the best possible use in service to you and mankind.

Thank you as always for your great help, Love, patients, kindness, and generosity.

Love,
Sign Your Name

How can I use my strengths to help achieve this goal?
I have great communication skills, I am a diplomat, a researcher, high interest in self-improvement, I'm a good speaker, I can write, I can teach, I have a desire to help others live the best life they can. I could use these skills to develop a business that helps other people achieve their highest potential.

What fills me with passion and purpose? How can I use my passion to achieve this goal?
Projects of my own design. Public situations. Self Help. Helping Others. Strategizing. I have to focus on developing a business that provides great value and benefit to others.

How can I use my skills in service to others and in pursuit of this goal?
Write books or self-help programs that can benefit others. Develop a marketing strategy for these programs that will reach the largest possible audience. Create and conduct seminars that will help others.

What other resources are available to help me reach this goal?
Money management strategies. I can focus on using what I already have more efficiently. I can invest an additional one hundred dollars per month. Reduce unneeded expenses by one hundred dollars per month. I can talk to a financial adviser to review my current investment strategy and look for ways to improve.

What people, organizations, books, training or any other services are available to help?
Other writers, publishers, agents, education experts, marketing experts, financial planners.

What is my timeframe to reach this goal?
3 to 10 years.

What specific tasks need to be accomplish in order to reach this objective?
Finish first book, complete chapters 15 through 20.
Solicit publishers
Look into self-publishing or Internet Web-Publishing
Develop a marketing strategy
Develop seminars that can be duplicated, run multiple seminars across the country.
Write second book and market.
Write third book and market.
Set appointment with financial expert for advice.
Identify unnecessary expenses and get rid of them.
Identify best place to invest an additional one hundred dollars per month.
Keep eyes open for money making opportunities and act quickly on them.

What do I see as the greatest obstacles to achieving this goal?
Time, a lot to do, doubt and negative self-limiting thinking.

What can I do to overcome these obstacles?
- Manage my time to get the tasks done quickly and in the best priority. Schedule at least 1 hour per day to work on these goal specific tasks. Work diligently every day to keep my mind focused on why I can accomplish this goal. Release my fears and doubts on a daily basis.
- Make sure the first book will be a best-seller packed full of value for every reader. Must be able to benefit a wide audience, be extremely marketable, be practical, fun, and powerful.
- Define a belief strategy to keep myself knowing I can do this. Remove doubt and fear quickly.
- Every chance I can I will enter a deep state of relaxation and visualize with great emotion and feeling that I already have wealth of over 1 million dollars.

How can I keep this goal in the front of my mind every day?
- I will work and believe as if this goal will take place and I will accept that my Higher Power knows what is best for me and that He will provide me with that. I can't lose. I will accept that He will give me what is best for me and everyone else involved. I know that this goal or something even better will come true.
- Every day I will read this Goal Achievement Strategy and dedicate time to work on it. At the same time I will review my strengths list and my passion and purpose list and strive to apply these things toward the achievement of this goal.
- Every day before sleep and upon wakening, I will relax for 5 minutes and intensely visualize the successful completion of this goal.
- I will look myself in the eyes (using a mirror of course) every day and confidently affirm that this desire is mine. I will repeat it over and over until I firmly believe it is possible, and when I truly believe it, I will find the way.

How far do you think a person would go using this strategy versus having no strategy at all? I think you've got it. Now be sure to complete a goal strategy for all the things you want or need most right now.

You don't have to begin working on them; just mapping them out on paper will get your subconscious mind working on fulfilling them. As far as pursuing and actively working on a goal, just pick your highest-ranking goal and focus on it first. When you have attained that goal, or when you feel you have enough time to pursue a second goal, pick the next highest ranking goal and get going on it.

Every day from this point on, ask yourself, "What can I do today to bring me closer to making this goal a reality." Exciting, focused, well-planned out goals are fun. They bring excitement and accomplishment into an otherwise meaningless existence. It's fun to set the course and start down the path of achievement.

Share Your Plans with Those Who Will Support You

Of course you'll probably want to share your excitement and passion with others because you're bubbling up from inside. Stop. There's one thing you need to be aware of in order to get the best possible support for reaching your dreams. Only tell positive people who will support you. Never tell negative people who won't.

Positive people will of course believe right alongside of you, they'll be pulling for you and for your success. You need to tell them and talk excitedly about your plans and dreams with them. This will keep the fire burning. On the flip side, negative people will not want you to succeed and will put doubt in your mind. Enough negative influence, fear and doubt, and you are sunk.

You don't need to look at why things can't be done. That's the job for people who want to remain ordinary. You are an inspirational superhero. Achieving the so-called impossible is your mission. You are of the same spirit as the Wright Brothers, Thomas Edison, and Henry Ford. You believe big, way bigger than the mass of humanity, and your accomplishments will be superhuman compared to theirs.

Overcome Procrastination

Superheros are always ready to spring into action. And why not, they have nothing to lose. They know their mission, they have the ability they need and they know they're going to get the job done. They have complete confidence so they just leap into action. No fear.

Sometimes this becomes a little difficult for us mortals. We avoid doing the things we know we should be doing for a variety of reasons. Unfortunately the very act of procrastination causes us to feel bad about ourselves. It delays accomplishing anything of value and causes us all sorts of problems.

Avoiding action really complicates things for us. It makes us feel guilty, inadequate, and lazy and it causes unnecessary stress as things begin to pile up. Be on guard so you can head off any urge to procrastinate. Take a look at the symptoms of procrastination listed below and see if you recognize any of them.

Symptoms of Procrastination

Substitution: Substituting one activity for another. When we are supposed to be accomplishing some objective or task, we suddenly decide to work on something else instead. Let's say we're supposed to be writing a term paper and all of the sudden we decide this is the opportune time to go shopping. What's wrong with this picture?

Over Explaining: Talking more about the task than actually doing it. Do you ever go around explaining to all your coworkers, family, friends and complete strangers the enormity of the task you are now faced with accomplishing. If you find yourself explaining the job at hand more than doing the job at hand you may have a problem.

Indecision: Let's see now which part of this objective should we start with. Maybe we should start here or maybe over there, let me think about this awhile. If a start here I will get this much done but it might be better to start over there because if I do, I might get that much done. Oh what's a person to do? Indecision is a real indication of procrastination.

Delay: Delay tactics used to be one of my personal favorites. If I just wait long enough maybe it will just go away. I'm sure most of us have had fun with this little game in one way or another. It sure seems silly when you get it in black and white.

Good Starter – Poor Finisher: A very common problem associated with inaction is to be a great starter but a poor finisher. Getting started is not a problem for me. I love to start new things. As long as I'm doing the part that interests me, I make good progress. However my mind only stays interested for so long. I can usually get halfway to three-fourths of the way done with almost anything. It's that last quarter that kills me.

Thomas Edison was like this too. Mr. Edison loved to start projects and then hand them off to someone else with the right expertise to finish the job. I suspect he was an idea man and that he really didn't care to do the details unless they interested him or unless he had to. He was very skilled in the art of finding people to work for him that could finish what he often started. That was a perfect solution within his ability to implement. I don't know about you but I don't have that same lot in life, I usually have to finish what I've started.

Writing this book is a perfect example. When I began to write this book I quickly made it through three-quarters of the way before slowing down. The last quarter was much slower than the rest of the course. For too many of us we not only slow down, we completely stop.

Unfortunately, stopping is the absolute worst thing we can do. It causes regret and dissatisfaction. Worse yet, if our objective was something that could have provided value to others, they also lose out.

The emotional freedom alone is worth getting things done. It's no longer some looming task hanging overhead, it becomes another accomplishment to add to a growing list. Eighty percent of the fun may be working towards a worthwhile goal, but if we don't finish the last twenty percent we can accumulate the baggage of unfinished business and regret.

Determine the Cause of Your Slow Down

Discovering the reason for inaction isn't difficult at all. You just need to ask yourselves a few probing questions to get to the core issues. Let's use the problem of getting through the last quarter of writing a book as an example. Here are a few questions you can ask yourselves to help pinpoint the problem.

- What sorts of things have I been doing to avoid this task?

Other projects, talking a lot about this great book instead of writing it, reviewing completed chapters and finding ways to rewrite them.

- Why am I really avoiding this task?

I guess I'm a little afraid it won't be of value. I fear it won't sell. I fear the changes that may happen if it does take off.

- What am I afraid of?

I'm afraid people will tell me it stinks and that all this time and effort will be for no good use.

- What am I trying to gain by avoiding this task?

Freedom from failure and rejection.

- What is the result of avoiding this work, what am I really getting?

A nagging feeling that I need to do this. I know I will always wonder if I could have done it. I know that there has to be at least some value to others. I feel like I am not reaching my potential and that if I don't complete it I will have failed without really giving it my all. Regret.

Answering these few questions will help you to understand why you're procrastinating. Some form of fear is usually at the core. Fear has ruined the aspirations of many a mortal. You need to get to the bottom of inaction and the quicker the better. The more time you waste pushing off the things you need to do, the worse you feel and the more unproductive you become.

Getting Moving Again

Once you have an idea of why you're putting things off you can find a solution to keep you moving. You can mentally ask Yourself the following questions to find a solutions.

- What do I need to do to complete this objective?

I need to get focused. I need to conduct research. I need to have a plan. I need to dedicate time. I need to make this a priority again. I need to make it fun as I really do enjoy writing. I need to get focused on all the benefits that will come from completing this book.

- What will I gain when I complete this, what will the benefits be for me?

I will be finally done and free to focus on the next accomplishment. I have completed something that can help others. I will have a deep sense of satisfaction. I will have a great summary reference of all the cool stuff I have learned in the process of writing this book. If the book becomes popular there could be some financial reward and other possible opportunities to serve greater numbers of people. I will understand what it takes to actually write a book and be better prepared to write the next one. After all how many people ever get this far?

- What will the value be to others when I complete this objective?

I hope it will help others to discover their great potential and understand the incredible value they bring to life. I hope others learn to use their incredible human abilities for enjoyment and to serve others. I hope people learn to develop a relationship with the Highest Power in the universe for guidance, direction, help and strength. I hope people will become free from the unnecessary things that hold them back. I hope people will realize a better life as a result of this book.

- How will I feel when it's done?

Free, a sense of accomplishment, good, satisfaction.

- What's the worst that can happen if I complete this objective?

The worst that could happen is that it wouldn't sell and that people wouldn't get value from it.

- What is the minimum I will get out of completing this objective?

A huge education. I will learn, test and apply powerful skills to improve my own life that will make me more valuable to others. I will learn what it takes to start a business and write a self-help program. I will have fun pursuing something I can get passionate about. I will grow, have fun, and enjoy having a purpose that is meaningful to me.

- What's the best that can happen if I complete this objective?

I help a lot of people and become famous and successful.

- What will happen if I don't complete this objective?

Regret. I will wonder if I could have made a difference.

- What steps can I take right now, what can I do to get this done?

Review outline of remaining chapters. Start one at a time. Commit to one chapter at a time 30 minutes a day. Just do it and have fun.

- Who can help me get this done?

Other writers, friends who believe in me, and my Higher Power.

- What other resources can I use to complete this?

Voice recognition software to speed up the writing process and make it fun and different.

Once you've returned your focus to the task at hand you can simply take the following steps to get the job done.

1. List each specific task that needs to be done from beginning to end.

2. Next to each difficult task write out a mini plan of action that will help you complete them and include any help you can enlist from others.

3. Commit blocks of time to work on each task.

4. Find a quiet place without distractions for working on your objectives during these time blocks.

5. Frequently visualize yourself completing the things you need to do and enjoying all the benefits of your accomplishment.

6. Every night before you go to sleep ask yourself the following question, how can I have fun, stay motivated, and get these things done?

Keep your mind focused on solutions and you'll find them. You can accomplish anything with the proper focus of your mind and your time. Answers will come and you will rise to the occasion. The rewards will far out-weigh any temporary inconvenience. Here are a few other things you can do to help you stay into action.

Think Your Way Into Action

A simple way to create a more positive focus is to quickly write out positive affirmations.

Repeatedly speaking or writing one-line sentences that say you can. If you speak them, say each statement 21 times and say it like you mean it. If you prefer to write, write each statement at least 7 times. Repetition helps build momentum. Here's an example...

I can accomplish this task.
I can provide my unique value in this situation.
I can get the help I need.
I can apply my skills and talents to this situation.
I can have fun with this project.
I can do a great job with this project.
I can get excited about this project.

Just speak or write positive statements over and over until you feel motivated to get going. This practice will take you into a more positive thought process about your work. It's fast, easy, and very effective.

Organize and Get Ready

Just getting set up is another way of activating yourself. Before you start working on a project, gather all the materials you need and get it all organized. That's all you commit to at first. Just getting the stuff set up. Once you get that far take a look at everything set up right before you. It's all ready, you might as well start. Try the five-minute thing and see how far you get by the end of the day.

Do These Things to Keep Your Mind in Positive Motion

- Avoid negative people, thoughts, and habits like the plague.
- Believe you will do what you've set out to do, tie in your passion wherever you can.
- Consider obstacles as normal life challenges and focus on the benefits of victory over them.
- Find something fun or create something fun in everything you have to do.
- Practice makes perfect so persist until you succeed.
- Desire as strongly as you can to complete the task at hand.
- Think about the consequences of not getting things done. Look at inaction as an enemy and commit to victory over it.
- Write letters or mentally ask your Higher Power for help to complete the task at hand.

Put your fears in the proper perspective. Not doing what you need to do, or what you really want to do has consequences. It keeps you in mediocre mode and puts your self-image at a level you don't want it to be. It makes you an average performer. I say average performer because procrastination is the problem of the masses. It doesn't make you evil or sub-human. It just makes you an average human being. And that's what we're trying to get beyond. We're working towards our highest potential.

As you've probably figured out by now, most procrastination problems can be fully avoided when you get to pick your own objectives. That's the great thing about working on your passion and purpose and using your strengths and unique value every day.

When you're in superhero mode using your unique value to serve others you already have motivation. When you're pursuing a goal of your own design you have drive and passion already. When you have passion and drive, procrastination is not much of a problem. Finding more time to do what you like is more of a problem. Commit at least a little time each day to pursuing your passion.

For now we are superheroes in an imperfect world. We have to do the best we can with what we have. So, while we still work for others and still have objectives and tasks to perform that are assigned by others, we can use what we've learned in this chapter to keep ourselves moving.

We can keep moving forward toward the fulfillment of our goals and dreams, performing at superhero levels compared to the normal mortals who still suffer from procrastination.

You are now ready for the final step in the SUPERMAN formula. You're ready to live each new day at your best for the rest of your life.

N – New Day Every Day
Chapter 13: "New Day Every Day – Discover The Easy Way To Ultimate Living A Day At A Time"

"You are what you repeatedly do. Excellence is not an event - it is a habit." - Aristotle 384-322 BC, Greek Philosopher and Scientist

Keep Life Exciting

Planning, anticipating, and working toward a worthwhile objective is indeed eighty percent of the fun. Don't' get me wrong, the last twenty percent is critical to complete, but we do often experience the greatest amount of pleasure during the first part of a pursuit. I've heard that many Olympic gold medalists experience quite a letdown after they achieve their goal. I can see why. They spend almost all of their lives perfecting their skills, becoming the absolute best they can be in their sport. They spend many hours every day working towards the dream of an Olympic gold medal.

They're driven by their dream, filled with excitement and anticipation of that glorious day. All that focus, energy, and work, enables them to reach their highest athletic potential. Their life is full of drive and purpose. Then the glorious day arrives and they win the gold medal. It's an awesome experience no doubt, but what's next? What will fill the newly created void?

Always remember to keep your life exciting by identifying your next passionate purpose. As you approach the completion of one goal, have the next one ready.

Reaching your superhuman potential is a process that continues for the rest of your life. Good thing! That way you're in for continued growth, advancement, fulfillment, and fun along the way. You will achieve many accomplishments and you'll always have the next objective ready to pursue once you've reached a specific objective.

Continually striving toward the next new thing will keep you positively charged. Your enthusiasm and excitement won't end because you'll be on a lifelong journey of anticipation.
Focus on Becoming Your Best

Focus is the key. We must keep our vision in the forefront of our thoughts throughout every moment of our waking day. Our dreams keep us motivated to stay the course. Much like other superhero's who have come before us, like Thomas Edison, Henry Ford, and the Wright Brothers. They weren't normal, definitely not average or ordinary by any means. Thank God they weren't!

Very few people believed in their big unrealistic dreams. I'm just glad that "they" did. At the end of the day, their accomplishments speak for themselves and so will yours. They changed the world and so will you as you make your life your mission. Live every moment at your best and you will accomplish great things.

Constantly seek opportunities to apply your talents, skills, and abilities. When an opportunity presents itself, leap into action. People won't usually object to your kindness or the value you add. In fact they'll usually say things like "why that so-and-so is really great, I wish more people were like that," "I wish I were more like that" or "so-and so is always right in the middle of making good things happen."

Your Destiny is Created Every Day by Your Actions

You need to focus on making at least a little progress every single day. Every day will either be used productively or it will become wasted time you can never get back. The term "New Day Every Day" means that you need to enjoy making progress towards your worthwhile goals, every day. It's not so daunting a task to be a superhero for one day, or even for a few moments throughout your day.

In this chapter you'll put together a workable daily routine that will ensure your days are the most rewarding and fulfilling they can be. The goal is to make your life as passionate, purposeful, exciting, fun, happy, and successful as is humanly possible. Every day!
Get Help from the Highest Power in the Universe

Seeking the help of your Higher Power is the perfect place to start. Before you continue it's time to write an emotionally charged, sincere letter, requesting help to develop a daily routine that will keep you on the superhero track.

Something along these lines...

Dear Higher Power,

I am confident that you want me to fulfill my highest potential. I am asking for your guidance, direction, protection, and help to become the greatest I can be. Help me to accomplish all that you would have me do in this life, so I can fulfill your great purpose for me.

Please grant me great wisdom, common sense, and good judgment in everything I do. Help me to focus on serving others with the gifts you have given me. Help me to focus on the right things and not to get side tracked with unworthy distractions. Please inspire me to develop a workable, practical, daily routine that will allow me to fulfill my greatest potential in service to you and mankind, one day at a time.

Thank you for your wisdom, help, guidance, and inspiration and thank you for the opportunity to serve in a greater capacity.

Love,
Sign Your Name.

That should get you off to a great start. Rest assured, if you do your part you will receive impressive help when you need it. When we're into positive action, using the abilities we've been blessed with to benefit others, we are almost always satisfied and happy. Keep your mind focused on the right things and develop a strong relationship with your Higher Power. Strive to do even a few worthwhile things each day and you will live an incredible life.

Your Powerful Daily Routine

What would you need to do each day to be at optimal performance? What would you need to do to fully enjoy each day and produce at your best? Let's take a look at incorporating the SUPERMAN Formula to do just that. Here are eight basic disciplines you will want to consider as you build your new way of life.

- **Superpower Awareness Discipline:** Stay aware of your incredible potential and the great power available to help you.

- **Uniqueness Discipline:** Find ways to use your strengths and weaknesses to benefit others.

- **Purpose & Passion Discipline:** Keep your passion and purpose in the front of your mind so your life is exciting.

- **Expertise of Superpowers Discipline:** Use your superpowers and your connection to your Higher Power in practical ways.

- **Release Discipline:** Release the enemies of fear, worry, guilt, anger, self-pity, and all negative thinking, daily.

- **Making a Difference Discipline:** Stay focused on how you can make a positive difference in this world.

- **Action Discipline:** Make yourself take continuous positive action, even when you're not in the mood.

- **New Day Every Day Discipline:** Experience each new day as if it is your last by making it your best.

Developing a little daily practice for each of these areas will significantly improve your life. Let's take a closer look at what you can do each day in each of these areas.

Superpower Awareness Discipline

Constantly be aware of the incredible power available to you. Make a daily habit of doing the following things.

Awaken each day with an attitude of gratitude. Be grateful that you've been given another day to live. Remember that each new day is a powerful gift from your Higher Power and commit yourself to using your time wisely.

All day long see the incredible power that is all around you. Everything you see was either made by man or by the great Creator. As you go about your day admire the trees, grass, sky, birds, sun, stars, animals and all the people you encounter.

Be mindful of the incredible power that sustains all these things. Be aware of all the human creations around you. The cars, streets, houses, TVs, stores, bridges, power lines, planes, cell phones, and so on. Let everything you see remind you of the incredible power that is all about you.

Think about how everything you see is made up of pulsating, vibrating, living energy, and how your own thoughts project energy waves that affect the things around you. Recognize the incredible power of human ideas, and thoughts, and the great transmitter and receiver that resides in every human mind. Recognize the need for access to your Higher Power for wisdom, guidance, direction and for supernatural intervention in times of need.

By keeping this perspective each day you will gain a great appreciation for the incredible possibilities that are available to you in this life.

Uniqueness Discipline

Unique value is what you have to offer the world. Make a daily habit of doing the following things.

Every morning and every evening briefly review your strengths list from Chapter 5. You could also post this list where you could see it throughout your day. This will help you to keep in mind all that you have to offer the world. Whenever you see an opportunity to use your gifts you will be ready to leap into action.

To avoid letting your weaknesses trip you up, review your weakness list from chapter 6 each morning. Always finish your review with your strengths list in order to stay positively focused.

Purpose and Passion Discipline

Focus your mind on your purpose and your passions will keep you driving ahead toward worthwhile pursuits. Make a daily habit of doing the following.

Review your purpose & passion statement from chapter 7 every day. Do this each morning as you awaken, and each evening before you go to sleep. You may want to post this list where you can see it frequently throughout the day. This will help you to stay focused on the good stuff and will give you the motivation you need to stay the course of pursuing your dreams.

Expertise of Superpowers Discipline

Practice using your human powers of mind over matter and intuition, and converse with your Higher Power every day. Make a daily habit of doing the following.

Every evening before you go to sleep spend at least five minutes intensely visualizing your primary goal. Fully experience your goal in your mind as if it were real, as if you had already achieved it. Feel what it would feel like; see it in as much detail as you are capable of. Also spend several minutes intensely visualizing yourself being the person you want to be. See, feel, and experience fully the person you truly desire to be. See yourself at your absolute best in different situations. Make it as real as you possibly can. If you can spend just five minutes each evening before you go to sleep on each of the use visualizations, you will be amazed at the results.

Throughout your day strive to be in touch with what your gut feelings are telling you. Constantly ask yourself, "What am I sensing?", "what am I feeling deep down?" Take a few minutes throughout each day to relax completely to a meditative state. While in a relaxed state ask questions about anything you desire, and then listen for answers. Also, while you're in this relaxed state, practice mentally projecting yourself into objects and sensing how they would feel, how they smell, whether they are light or dark, and so on. This exercise will help to sharpen your intuitive abilities.

Every day make contact with your Higher Power. Either write a brief letter or say an intense prayer asking for guidance, direction, wisdom, common sense, good judgment, and for help to be at your best. Ask your Higher Power to help you do his will ahead of your own. Ask him to take this new day into his care and to work out all details so that everything will work out in the best interest of all people involved.

Ask for inspiration and help to accomplish great things and to be a shining example wherever you go. Ask your higher power to work in the minds of others in order to grant you great favor in their site, and ask for inspiration to use your abilities to serve and help others in a meaningful way. Trust that your Higher Power will help you to accomplish the things that are best for you and everyone else.

Release Discipline

Release your internal enemies of fear, worry, guilt, regret, arrogance, self-pity, bitterness, resentment, doubt, and envy on a daily basis in order to prevent dangerous buildup. Make a daily habit of doing the following.

Before starting each day right out a quick "what's bugging me now?" list. Just quickly write down all the things that are bothering you, anything that's on your mind. Get your negative thinking out in the open so you can see it for what it is. Let go of the things you have no control over and take positive steps where you can. Forgive yourself for your mistakes and forgive others for theirs. If you have been wrong, quickly admit it and make amends where you can. This will keep your conscience clear, allowing your mind to operate at peak performance.

Making a Difference Discipline

Make a difference in the world around you by being different than the world around you. Make a daily habit of doing the following.

Smile at every person you meet and treat them as the important people they are. Do the little things that make a big difference. Open doors for people, be kind, be positive, be generous, and strive to bring out the best in others. Little things make a big difference.

Action Discipline

Continuous action is critical to progress and fulfillment. Make a daily habit of doing the following.

Review your goal achievement strategy. Keep it where you can see it or review it constantly. Be on the lookout for signs of procrastination and get to the core of the problem quickly. Review the chapter on action if you need help. Do whatever it takes to get going again. Your time is your life, don't waist a single minute of it. Remember the consequences of putting things off.

New Day Every Day Discipline

Now at this point you're probably thinking, how in the world can I get all of these things done in the limited time I have. Don't worry; this is where we put it all together in a practical form so you can live each day as a new exciting and rewarding day. Let's simplify things and put together a sample daily schedule that includes the disciplines listed above so you can see what the whole thing really looks like. Keep in mind, this is your workable daily routine. Every person's routine will be different. The idea is to include as many of the ideal disciplines as you can into your day.

Sample Daily Discipline Schedule:

Time	Discipline	Min
7:00 AM	Communicate with Higher Power asking for guidance, direction and protection for the day. Ask for understanding of his will for you and power and willingness to carry that out.	5 Min

7:30 AM	Listen to positive attitude or self help audio's as you drive to work.	0 Extra Time
8:00 AM	Review strengths, weaknesses, passion and purpose summary statements. Review goal achievement strategy. Write quick, one line "I am" positive affirmation statements. Write out a quick "what's bugging me now" list.	10 Min
9:00 AM		
10:00 AM		
11:00 AM		
12:00 PM	Review strengths, weaknesses, passion and purpose statements. Communicate with your Higher Power asking for any help you may need.	10 Min
1:00 PM		
2:00 PM		
3:00 PM		
4:00 PM		
5:00 PM		
6:00 PM	Listen to positive attitude tapes or self help tapes as you drive home.	0 Extra Time
7:00 PM		

8:00 PM		
9:00 PM		
10:00 PM	Write out all the things that bothered you during the day and why. List anyone you need to make amends to.	10 Min
10:30 PM	Relax and visualize the upcoming day in great detail. See yourself at your best in every type of situation. Desire to have a great day.	5 Min
	Total Investment of Time in Minutes	**40 Min**

Notice in this example the maximum amount of time we dedicated to any of these daily disciplines was 10 minutes, and only 5 to 10 minutes at a time sprinkled throughout the rest of the day. We logged no time for listening to positive attitude or self help audio's because we used drive time where we couldn't be doing anything else anyway.

There's a lot of positive power packed into 40 minutes of this day. There's still time to sleep, work, and there's time left to your discretion. You will want to commit at least 1 hour per day to actively pursue your dreams. Using the techniques in this book your waking time will be significantly more productive and powerful than ever before.

Setting up a daily discipline that works for you only requires a small investment of time up front and a minimal daily investment divided up into little chunks. Use your time wisely, invest in yourself, it will pay big dividends for you and for those you benefit as a result.

Make the Process Efficient & Effective

Once you've got your daily discipline mapped out, use it until you need to change it. As you grow and develop you can add and subtract to keep things fresh.

Once you add these daily disciplines to your life you will automatically start employing more and more of the powerful skills you've learned. Tremendous gains will be made. These simple but powerful daily disciplines will help to ensure that you never stop pursuing excellence.

You just need to plan a little success into your day as part of your routine. You don't even have to dedicate an enormous amount of time to your superhero pursuit, just a few minutes here and there sprinkled throughout your long day. With repetition your daily practice will become a habit.

Live to Give and Reap the Rewards

There are really only two paths to follow in life, the way of giving and the way of getting. Giving of ourselves produces rewards, happiness, peace and success. Striving to get from others leaves us empty, unsatisfied and a failure. No matter how much stuff we accomplish or accumulate by getting, we will never be full. Selfishness has no lasting or meaningful satisfaction. The only way to be full is to give, emulating the way a superhero lives.

You are a unique and wonderful creation. You have incredible abilities and value to offer the world. You have access to the greatest power in the universe for affecting positive change. You have acquired the knowledge and skills that will enable you to live up to your superhuman potential. Congratulations and welcome to the elite class of superheroes.

May you be richly blessed in all your pursuits, and may you be blessed with great wisdom, common sense, good judgment, great character, material, physical, mental and spiritual wealth, along with great happiness and success!

To your Super-Success and Beyond!

Mark Duin
www.markduin.com
www.careersuccesstraining.com

BIBLIOGRAPHY

Reference Material:

- Auerbach, Loyd, "Mind Over Matter." Kensington, May 1996.

- Capra, Fritjof, "The TAO of Physics." Shambhala, 2000.

- Carnegie, Dale, "How to Win Friends and Influence People." Pocket Books, November 1998.

- Covey, Stephen R., "The 7 Habits of Highly Effective People.", Fireside, 1990.

- Finley, Thomas K, "Mental Dynamics." Prentice Hall, 1991.

- Hill, Napoleon, "Think and Grow Rich." Fawcett Crest, May 1988.

- Lakein, Alan, "How To Get Control Of Your Time And Your Life." A Signet Book, June 1974.

- McGill, Ormond, "The New Encyclopedia of Stage Hypnotism." Crown House Publishing Company Limited. 2001.

- McMoneagle, Joseph, "Mind Trek." Hampton Roads Publishing Company, Inc. 1997.

- Murphy, Dr. Joseph PhD, "The Power of Your Subconscious Mind." Bantam Books, January 2001.

- Ostrander, Sheila and Schroeder, Lynn with Ostrander, Nancy, "Superlearning 2000." A Dell Book, August 1997.

- Scheinfeld, Robert, "The Invisible Path to Success." Invisible

Path Publishing, 2000

- Schwartz, David J. PhD, "The Magic of Thinking BIG." A Fireside Book, May 1987.

- Stine, Jean Marie, "Super Brain Power." Prentice Hall, 2000.

- Talbot, Michael, "The Holographic Universe." Harper Perennial, 1992.

- Targ, Russell, and Katra, Jane, PhD, "Miracles of Mind." New World Library, 1999.

- Zukav, Gary, "The Dancing Wu Li Masters." Bantam Books, August 1980.

- Ziglar, Zig, "See You At The Top." Pelican Publishing Company, 2005.

About The Author

Mark Duin is a former drug addict and 9th grade dropout. Today Mark is part of the Management Team for a multimillion dollar Technology Business.

Despite facing enormous life challenges Mark has discovered the way to a successful rewarding life. He has a successful corporate career, a successful marriage of over 24 years, financial success, and is an award winning speaker and internationally recognized author.

He is an acknowledged expert on overcoming challenges and on maximizing human potential. Mark combines spiritual principles, success principles, accelerated learning, and advanced personal development methods to enable people to live the best life possible!

Talented, inspirational, warm, funny and profound, Mark is a motivational speaker who addresses a variety of topics relating to business, career, and personal success.

Meet Mark at www.markduin.com and grab valuable free training that will help you enjoy an extraordinary life of passion and purpose!

www.ingramcontent.com/pod-product-compliance
Lightning Source LLC
Chambersburg PA
CBHW071706090426
42738CB00009B/1684